The Cross
And Weeping Still

By Vertis Kincaid Jimerson

† The Cross And Weeping Still †

Copyright © 2015
By Vertis Kincaid Jimerson
The Cross and Weeping Still
Printed in the United States of America
ISBN 978-0-9864305-3-4

All rights are reserved solely by the author.
The author declares that the contents are original and do not infringe on the rights of any other person.

No part of this book may be reproduced in any form except with permission from the author. The views in this book are not necessarily the views of the publisher.

About The Author

I, Vertis Kincaid Jimerson, the author of this book, was born July 22, 1941. My parents were Wallace and Grozella Kincaid. They were from Louisville, Mississippi. My daddy was a coal miner and my mother, for the most part, a housewife. Occasionally, she did "day work," and worked some at a school in the janitorial department. I have four siblings--two brothers and two sisters.

I attended McCaw Elementary School and Western-Olin High School in Birmingham, Alabama. The same school attended by Paul Williams and Eddie Kendricks of the Temptations singing group. I also finished Grady Memorial Hospital School of Nursing in Atlanta, Georgia, and worked as a Registered Nurse (R.N.) for nearly 40 years.

In 1963, I married Raymond Jimerson, and to that union three sons were born-- Raymond, Jr., 1964; Juan, 1966; and Kevron, 1972. My husband and I worked hard. We built our home in Hueytown, Alabama, and moved in years later, after paying as we built. My husband has a Bachelor of Science (B.S.) degree, majoring in Chemistry, from Tennessee State University. When we married he went back to school to obtain an education in air conditioning and refrigeration to increase the family income. My sons were obedient and never caused trouble. I often think I never had to visit a jail to see a son or bond one out. I thank God for this fact.

When Raymond died, the two older sons were attending Tennessee State University, and the youngest was a student at Pittman Jr. High School. Presently, all three sons are employed: one as an engineer; one a car salesman; and the other in the Cardiac Department at the University of Alabama Hospital.

I have two biological grandchildren (Kevron, Jr., Joshua) and two other grandchildren through marriage (Narnesha, Bryanna). I also have one biological great grandchild (Laila M. Jimerson).

I never remarried, but have dated one man (Vincent Burrell, Sr.) for over 20 years. I attend the First Baptist Church, Fairfield, Alabama, still with much biblical understanding and love.

† The Cross And Weeping Still †

Acknowledgements

I give praise and thanks to the LORD, Jesus Christ,
for the dreams, insight, and strength to write this book.

For insistence that I read and study, I applaud my parents Wallace and Grozella Kincaid.

To the great teachers at McCaw Elementary School (formerly South Pratt), Western/Jackson-Olin High School (formerly Western-Olin), both of Birmingham, Alabama, and Grady Memorial Hospital School of Nursing in Atlanta, Georgia, I'm grateful.

To Dr. Bernard Kincaid, my brother, typist, and computer whiz, I'm thankful.

To the many great doctors, nurses, and therapists at Baptist Princeton Hospital and University Hospital, both in Birmingham, Alabama, and Lloyd Noland Hospital in Fairfield, Alabama, for all the hard work, thank you.

For encouragement and support from my children, friends, in-laws, and other relatives, I love you all.

For Effie Smith, my husband's private nurse, I'll never forget you.

To my church members, at First Baptist Church, Fairfield, Alabama, and the former minister and his wife, thank you.

For Alfred, Raymond's brother, thanks for cutting his hair and shaving him weekly—that uplifted his spirits.

For everyone who helped me in any way to accomplish my goal of completing this book, thank you so much.

Table Of Contents

About the Author II

Introduction V

Chapter 1: Occurrences of Life – Mama's Death: August 1983 1

Chapter 2: Beginning of Husband's Illness with Progression: August 1984 5

Chapter 3: Treatments for Raymond (husband) – My Life as a Wife, Mother and Nurse. Preparation for Christmas 1985. Started Diary 9

Chapter 4: Post-Holiday Celebration; Beginning of New Year and Occurrences of Next Few Months 19

Chapter 5: Hospitalization of Raymond (May) and Post-Hospitalization: 1986 41

Chapter 6: Hospitalization for Neck Problems (July) and Post-Surgery 55

Chapter 7: Hospitalization: August 5 – 15, 1986, and Post-Care 63

Chapter 8: Hospitalization: September 18, 1986, and Post-Care 71

Chapter 9: Hospitalization: November 9 – 30, 1986, and Death 81

Things I've Learned From Theses Experiences! Things I Want You To Know 91

Addendum: Lab Studies And Progress Notes 92

Introduction

(written August 3, 1987)

This book is written by divine guidance in memory of my late husband, Raymond Jimerson, Sr. It is about his two-year struggle with prostate cancer that metastasized (or spread) to the bones--and possibly the brain. The purpose of the book is to give the reader some insight into the problems, needed care, and emotional impact on both family and friends of a person suffering with this malady.

It is inspired divinely in as much as I [the author] was sleeping and was told to write it by [in] a dream. In the dream, I [the author] was trying to select an actor to play Raymond on Broadway, and I came up with Bernard, my brother, a faculty member at the University of Alabama in Birmingham. He also is a Director of a program there.

Even the color of the book (white with pinkish red roses around the border) was revealed to me. It is with reluctance that I write it because many secrets will be divulged, and we were a somewhat "private" family. Money obtained from the sale of this book will be divided among charities, the American Heart Association and, especially, the American Cancer Society.

For I feel much research still is needed to find a cure for this most dreaded disease. Sometimes I feel I am without my husband, who died at age 54 years, so others could benefit from this tragedy. If so, his living and his suffering was not all in vain. I am not a stranger to cancer and suffering, since [because] I have been a Registered Nurse since 1963. But, what I learned the last two years was first-hand.

It was from two sides, I was able to witness it: as a professional nurse and as a wife. We had three sons together: Raymond, Jr., born August 13, 1964; Juan, born January 20, 1966; and Kevron, born February 8, 1972. The two older boys attend Tennessee State University, Nashville, Tennessee. This was also Raymond, Sr.'s alma mater. Kevron is a student at Pittman Junior High School, Hueytown, Alabama.

Chapter One

OCCURRENCES OF LIFE – MAMA'S DEATH
(started August 1983)

"*Ashes to ashes, dust to dust*"-- the words cut like a knife. For today, August 11, 1983, the dear, tender friend, Mama was laid to rest. The poor diabetic, taking insulin twice daily, who had a heart that was greatly enlarged, and who had an arrhythmia, ventricular tachycardia, or heart disorder that wouldn't respond to any medication. She died Monday, after becoming ill on the way home from the hospital Saturday. You see, it started when she became confused and had hypoglycemia, or a low blood sugar.

She was admitted to Community Hospital, a small hospital, and later transferred to Lloyd Noland Hospital after she complained of pain in her right side, and had a fever. Some time ago she had been hospitalized at Lloyd Noland Hospital with an appendix problem, and abscess and intestinal obstruction. So, her present doctor transferred her to Lloyd Noland Hospital where her former doctor worked.

After discharge from Lloyd Noland Hospital on a very hot day, she blacked out enroute home and again after she got home. My brother, Leon, worked on her, called an ambulance and paramedics. I administered mouth-to-mouth resuscitation, and later a Code 10 (an emergency cry for medical help) was called in the Emergency Room. She survived, and was transferred to the Cardiac Care Unit where she lived a couple of days. Many codes were called, and many emergency treatments were given.

On Monday morning at 1:17 a.m., she died. An autopsy, of the chest only, was performed. This was a bleak moment in my life--a very bleak moment. You see, this mother was a woman I had in my mind nominated as Mother of the Year, of the World, and Mother of the Universe. She had raised five children, the oldest, me, was 15 years old when my father died. She had sent all of us through high school.

Bernard, my brother, had achieved the highest academic level of a Ph.D. degree; Leon, a masters degree; Barbara, the youngest, a B.S. degree in Biology. Velera had taken a business course, and I had finished Grady Memorial Hospital School of Nursing, and worked at the time as a Registered Nurse 20 years. Mama had accomplished this with only a small wooden home, a Social Security monthly check, and working odd jobs in school lunchrooms, day work, and praying very hard.

She never spent a night away from us children, never drank alcohol, or used profanity. Any male suitor that came to our home, sat on the front porch or living room, and behaved like a gentleman--and they were few. Now it has all ended. A part of me ended too. I sought to blame her death on my car's air conditioner not being cold enough, or my driving too fast to get her home from the hospital. But none of this brought Mama back. I tried to stop my sister from crying after her death while in the Cardiac Care Waiting Room, by telling her Mama was a dignified woman and in essence wouldn't approve of her behavior.

The grieving process for me was slow and painful. Mama, dear Mama, had left me. But little did I know what was awaiting me. This was only the beginning of occurrences in August.

Chapter Two

BEGINNING OF HUSBAND'S ILLNESS – WITH PROGRESSION
(started August 1984)

In August 1984, one year after burying my dear mother, Raymond, my husband of nearly 21 years was weak, having some back discomfort, and bouts with hesitation and difficulty in passage of urine. I mean when trying to urinate sometimes it was hard to start, and after starting it would stop. In a few minutes he'd have to return to the bathroom to try again. His blood count (hemoglobin and hematocrit) was below normal. So his doctors admitted him to the hospital for tests. Included in the tests was a bone marrow aspiration that confirmed what the doctors had feared. Cancer cells in the marrow, a sign of bone metastasis, most probably from the prostate gland, they told me.

The doctors gave him a drug, Stilbesterol, one mg. by mouth after discharge. This medication is a hormone that depresses the action of the prostate gland, slowing down the cancerous process. I asked the doctors to give him a blood transfusion to build him up; for I hated to see him weak and dragging, sometimes looking pale. But, they agreed to give him iron tablets by mouth instead. They said it would slowly build his blood count. I was searching for a get-well quick treatment; Raymond had always been healthy. The iron tablets caused him great distress, because they caused constipation and some stomach distress. So, in addition to the iron tablets and Stilbesterol, he now needed to add an antacid for his stomach and a stool softner to help with the bowel elimination.

I was not allowed to tell the children what was happening. Some close family members knew. Life for the most part was normal as usual. Raymond and I both worked. He, at U.S. Steel, Fairfield Works most of the time, and I at Lloyd Noland Hospital, Fairfield, Alabama. We went to church regularly at First Baptist Church, Fairfield. We ate well, enjoyed life as best we could. Somehow, though, I couldn't have fun. My thoughts always wandered back to Raymond, what the future held, how long he would or wouldn't live.

The doctors that diagnosed his problem would not put a time limit on his life. They would say, "he might live for years." I was too afraid to do much reading or research on this subject of prostate cancer. I lived day-by-day full of hope that the diagnosis was in error, that the Lord would miraculously heal him so we could travel about and tell of this great healing. O, I prayed and prayed. He kept his regularly scheduled doctors appointments and took his medication religiously. If he left one dose at home, he'd discover it before I left for work and call me to bring it by his job, as I went to work.

I was burdened and cried a lot, mostly in church. Still going through the grief over the loss of Mama, and now coping with this cancer of the prostate --my, my!

Chapter Three

TREATMENT FOR RAYMOND (HUSBAND) – MY LIFE AS A WIFE, MOTHER AND NURSE. PREPARATION FOR CHRISTMAS 1985

(Started Diary)

So, in December 1985, I started a diary. In the diary I wrote: "I hesitate to start a story after so much emotional, traumatic, informative parts will be left out due to not writing it day-by-day, but maybe, it'll work," I wrote. "I'll start a report daily or every few days--now!"

Wednesday, December 11, 1985

I went to see my doctor at Lloyd Noland Hospital today. He is a fine, young internist. I went because I felt uncomfortable in the chest. He took an electrocardiogram (EKG) that was reported as normal. He said my heart sounds were normal on auscultation (as he listened with the stethoscope). He stated that in his opinion, my problem was related to stress. He then wanted to know if this was work- or home-related. I replied "home-related." He then joked, "Oh, work is a piece of cake, huh?" I explained that my husband had prostatic cancer, with metastasis. I told him I thought that it might be helpful if I write a book on dealing with Raymond's problem. He encouraged this mightily. I think he thought writing might be therapeutic, a stress-release mechanism.

This same afternoon, Raymond saw an orthopedist at Lloyd Noland Hospital because of pain in his left leg. After x-rays were done, he concluded that Raymond had further spread of cancer (or metastasis) and probably needed more radiation therapy. You see, Raymond's primary physicians and oncologists are at another hospital, where he received radiation for bone pain before now, and also low doses of radiation prior to starting Stilbesterol treatment by mouth. You see, Stilbesterol, which is a hormone, can cause men to have large breasts like women. Radiation therapy reduces the breast growth.

Raymond was further advised by the orthopedist at Lloyd Noland Hospital not to work until returning to the primary Radiologist, who gave him radiation in the past. However, this doctor is presently on vacation and will not return until Monday. X-rays taken at Lloyd Noland Hospital were taken by hand to Baptist Hospital-Princeton by Raymond after proper "release" papers were signed. This cast a gloomy spell on impending Christmas plans, but I must push forward.

Thursday, December 12, 1985

I called Ray, Jr. and Juan to see if they received the $20 I sent them to come from Nashville, Tennessee. They will drive. In Nashville, there is snow in the forecast. So, they want to come home tonight. But this worries me. I know they probably are tired after attending class, packing clothes, etc. I keep thinking about the car wreck my father had in 1948. He went to sleep driving from Louisville, Mississippi, to Birmingham, Alabama after becoming real tired. So, I encouraged them to wait until Friday, and that's what they did. I called early Friday morning to seek the status of things. Ray, Jr. answered me on the phone saying "I don't know" when I asked if it was snowing. I said sternly, "Look out and see." Then he noted that it wasn't.

When I got home from work, they were home. I had done some last minute Christmas shopping and grocery shopping before coming home. It's amazing how much a 20-year old, a 19-year old, and a 13-year old who is 46 inches in the waist, can eat. But today is payday, and I've prayed as I always do for God to stretch my paycheck and relieve my heart of worry, trying to pay bills and Christmas shop at the same time.

Saturday, December 14, 1985

I had my hair washed and set today, dried clothes in the Laundromat, after going to Forestdale to find a Colecovision set that Kevron desperately has been trying to find for Christmas. Raymond paid for it, by giving me a check. In going to Forestdale, and being tired due to putting up Christmas decorations, cleaning the house, and other wifely duties, I made a left turn into a wrong lane of oncoming traffic. This scared both Kevron and me. I feel nervous.

Kevron, my youngest son, criticized my driving and voiced his opinion about his belief of my losing my eyesight. I became more upset and blurted out, "You know your daddy is dying. That's why I make so many mistakes." Afterwards, on the way home, he questioned me on why I said that. I lied and said, "You know your daddy is sick." He asked, "Do you know something you're not telling me?" "Is daddy going to die?" I replied, "Everyone is going to die, and only God knows when. Now, don't worry me."

Sunday, December 15, 1985

Raymond got up, showered and shaved, and went to church (late, of course). This quality in him has always worried and annoyed me. He isn't concerned about timing. But, my mother taught punctuality as I grew up, so did the Methodist church I grew up in. A few years ago, I became a member of the Baptist church to keep my family worshipping together. I listened on the radio to the church services at First Baptist, where Raymond, Sr. was attending today. The minister preached an enlightening message regarding wise men.

He stressed that the Bible did not say there were three wise men or ten, nor were their names given. I listened intently as I cooked a delicious dinner of fresh turnip greens, beef roast, white potatoes cooked in jackets, cornbread, and fresh peach cobbler pie. Raymond, Sr. had frozen these peaches two years ago. We drank cola that I had bought Friday as the beverage. I had spent a total of $89.00 for groceries. Already one gallon of milk was gone. I've always let the children eat as desired, but pray that I would have enough money to feed them in a manner that they're accustomed to eating during these times.

Early this morning my sister Barbara called and woke me up and talked at length, apologizing for any intrusion. She has been so sick with pseudo tumoroid cerebri. She still grieves over Mama's death, and clings to me like glue. I believe it's because I'm beginning to look more like Mama, and have her exact voice. Today, I'm anxious about tomorrow, Monday. Raymond is to see the doctor--a determination regarding metastasis, working, and other things. [Working depends on what the doctor says.] He is to take the x-rays taken earlier at the hospital where I work with hm.

I recap these things in my mind: Raymond's cancer was diagnosed August 1984. He was again hospitalized August 1985 after bouts with severe back pains and decreased appetite. He was discharged September 14, 1985. Radiation was started in the hospital, and was to be continued on an out-patient basis. The first determination was 10 radiation treatments, but was extended to 13 to get the necessary dosage. These treatments made him nauseous and weak. So now, I dread tomorrow, Monday, because more radiation treatments might be necessary. Monday came and went: the result was markings on his abdomen and left leg made by the doctor in the Oncology Department. Radiation treatments are to resume tomorrow at 4:00 p.m.

Tuesday, December 17, 1985

Today at work for me was mostly routine. I saw four patients and obtained nursing assessments. We exchanged gifts, since we had pulled names earlier. My boss, the Director of the Eldercare Program, had my name. We had posted a suggestion list (or desire list) earlier, and she bought me pink and white Dearfoam shoes and a plant for my office. I gave the person whose name I had pulled an am/fm clock radio. She seemed proud.

A party with my co-workers is to be tonight at the boss' townhouse in Hoover. I had mixed emotions about going to the party because of two reasons: First, I'm the only black in the department of six. I'm called "chocolate pud" by one of my co-workers whose husband is to drive all of the employees of the western section to the party. She has mentioned that he does not like Mr. T or Tina Turner, both black entertainers. I didn't know how he'd feel driving me to the party.

I supplied a meat tray with another co-worker chipping in for help. Secondly, I didn't go to the party because Raymond had his first radiation treatment of this series today. I feared he might have nausea, depression, and other side effects. He watched TV staring blankly most of the time. He ate a good supper of pinto beans, cornbread, turkey necks, and coke. He went to bed at 8:30 p.m. He is sleeping soundly by 9:30 p.m., with his eyes partially open. He looks momentarily like he is dying--to a nurse of 20 plus years. I can't help but wonder if this will be his last Christmas.

I bought another poinsettia today, now totaling three. I can't buy new furniture, hire the cleaning to be done, but I can decorate what I have the best I can. A small Santa lights up the living room, small candle decorations adorn the dining room table, small wax Santas and other decorations adorn the foyer table. Two poinsettias are on each side of the TV in the basement. Five stockings with all of our names are on the fireplace in the basement. The Christmas tree nearby has bows, lights, and about five white doves. I now think about the impending Christmas party to be held at our home Sunday. The Jimerson family and a few friends were invited as they were last year. Now I start frantically thinking what will I serve? Will Raymond feel like this: Is it my last family Christmas gathering? Oh God!, I pray, be merciful please.

✝ The Cross And Weeping Still ✝

Wednesday, December 18, 1985

Raymond had radiation treatment number two of this series. It seems to drain him. He is having quite a bit of leg pain tonight. I sent Ray, Jr. to the drugstore for a refill of the Darvocet N prescribed for him, but it was closed. Ray, Jr., now desperate, tried another drugstore (same chain) that was open to get the pain medication. The pharmacist did not fill the prescription, because he had no way of checking numbers, original prescription dates and other things pharmacists must do to refill prescriptions. Another pain medication, Hydrocodone, is in the house, but Raymond is reluctant to take it because it causes him to be constipated.

Raymond's car stopped running today--a bad alternator. His station wagon has no heat, and he has been promising to fix it himself. I warned him that pneumonia could be fatal if contracted. He paid Juan's tuition to Tennessee State University, nearly $2,500, due December 20th. I borrowed $1,500 to pay Ray, Jr.'s. He is getting a student loan of about $1,200 that's to be repaid after graduation also. Kevron's mid-semester grade in science is "F," and I cautioned him to pick himself up when down, when he asked me "Why do people get down sometimes?" (referring to a depressed feeling). The "F" paper had to be signed by a parent, so I signed it. His other grades were fairly good.

Raymond ate meatballs, collard greens, leftover pinto beans, and cornbread for dinner. He asked, "What is there to drink,?" and I answered "water." I honestly forgot that I bought two large root beer drinks yesterday.

About 10:00 p.m. I carried root beer to the bedside for him, and put the Hydrocodone on the bedside table, hoping desperately that he would take it. Raymond is stubborn sometimes and rebels if pushed. So, I left it hoping that he would be motivated to take it. Before I went to sleep, Raymond's sister called to inquire about Sunday's family gathering. She suggested that I serve hors d'oeuvres, but I quickly suggested bar-b-cue. Later, I wished I had gone along with her idea. Pressures mount and I keep thinking--"Tell me not in mournful numbers, life is but an empty dream." I must retire now and prepare for tomorrow's work.

Thursday, December 19, 1985

Today I went to the Methodist church where senior citizens meet weekly. This is all part of my job. The doors were locked--somehow it was not communicated to me that they would be closed until January 2, 1986. So, I went back to the hospital, saw a patient; thus, obtaining a complete health history that is to be forwarded to the doctor. Later I went to West End Senior Citizens site and took blood pressures, counseling when necessary.

I later called home and asked Ray, Jr. to take a chicken out of the freezer so that it could be cooked for supper. He forgot to do it, and called back home after leaving and told Kevron to do it. Needless to say, when I got home the chicken was still frozen, and my feet and legs were tired. I had worn heels to work and dressed a little differently, so I could attend a "work" party after duty hours. The hostess is a lovely white lady that volunteers to help ElderCare. Her home is beautiful, and she is a gracious hostess that prayed with me and hugged me before I left. All of my co-workers, a doctor and his aide from the hospital came also. So, I went to sleep after work allowing the chicken to thaw. It was 8:00 p.m. before I got up, fried the chicken, cooked boxed macaroni and cheese, and drank cola.

Raymond ate leftover greens, and retired early, using a heating pad and pain pills to alleviate pain. When asked if he had gotten his prescription for pain medication filled, he answered "yes, yes, yes" (as if he's tired of my inquiring). He heard me call my friend, Brenda, and invite her to the Christmas party to be held Sunday at our home. He later asked me who was coming and how many people would be invited. He said, "I thought it was a family affair." He's concerned about seating accommodations. He mentioned renting chairs for the affair. I'm concerned because the bricks on the front porch are loose and need cement, but he says it can't be done in this cold weather. Kevron, the youngest, is studying with my persuasion and threat that he'd better not bring any "F's" home on his report card again.

Friday, December 20, 1985

Before I left for work, Raymond was lying in bed, watching me dress for work and said, "Well, sir, you've gotten slick. I called the hospital to talk to you yesterday and they told me that you were taking a vacation day." Now, I know this was a lie. I had many witnesses of how hard I worked on the field and at the hospital. I believe this statement came about as frustration on his part--frustration that he tries to impart to me seemingly. Today we had a party at the hospital, that was nice. Also, turkeys were given to all employees today. My co-worker had corsages from the Head Injury Alliance that she and I distributed to new mothers (only three) and the elderly of Wing 2B at the hospital.

I called home before getting off duty and Raymond stated that the house was clean, so clean I'd hardly know it--the kitchen floor had the dark spots removed, the foyer was clean, and the countertops in the kitchen were clean. He always emphasized any housework he did, sometimes exaggerating. So, I didn't know what to expect when I got home. Before hanging up, he told me that he'd be shopping when I got off. I asked "What kind of shopping?" He said, "Grocery and gift shopping." I guess they went to get me a gift, but there were no groceries when I got home.

So, I didn't wash the kitchen curtains as I planned because there was not any flour to make flour starch that I use on them. When he did come home, he came with his belt loosened, and in a big hurry. I asked, "What's the matter?" He said, "I've messed in my clothes." The doctor had explained that radiation in the present area would probably cause diarrhea, and it had. Kevron ran into the house before Raymond, very excitedly. This whole thing seemingly is working on him emotionally. When I asked Kevron what was wrong, he said, "nothing," but in came Raymond and I knew. Raymond went to bed early, but Ray, Jr. came home and told him about Scrooge being on TV, so Raymond got up and watched TV with the children. The children and his mother, Sarah, who died in January 1982, were always "his life." He gave them a total commitment.

No radiation was given Raymond today, the machine at the hospital isn't functioning, and they are off on weekends. So, Raymond is to check back Monday. Raymond and Kevron ate at Quincy's Restaurant today. However, I fried a package of ocean perch fish after getting home. But before coming, I stopped and purchased ribs for bar-b-cueing, bread, Christmas cookies, and something to make red punch so it will be decorative. All in preparation for the party Sunday.

Sunday, December 22, 1985

The Christmas party was nice. The house was beautifully decorated, the food was delicious, and plentiful. (Bar-b-cue ribs; baked beans; potato salad; slaw; Christmas cookies, including fruit cake cookies; a cheese ball; crackers; peanuts; potato chips; bar-b-cue bread; egg nog; and two bowls of red punch.) The guests were predominately family. Friends included Brenda and her husband, Joe; Effie and Eevie; Mable and Bernice, who are close friends of the Jimerson family. Harold, Raymond's nephew, and Sharon, Raymond's niece, were conspicuously absent. "Mae Mae," who is Raymond's brother's mother-in-law, came. She looked pretty, and was escorted back home by Juan, our second oldest son. She was the oldest person present, and everyone made a fuss over her. Now,

I feel Christmas has come and gone. I don't have spirit to get up and cook for Christmas like I normally do. I will, however, bake a cake, potato pies, cook a turkey and ham for Christmas, later.

Raymond announced immediately after returning from church, and hours before the Christmas party, "There wasn't a dry eye in the church today, including mine." I know he had vented his feelings, and I replied nonchalantly, "There's nothing wrong with that." While he was at church, a friend of his family, Bama, came by with a card and Aramis cologne for him. She brought this by early because she would not be able to come to the party due to another engagement at Ruby's house, an ex-co-worker of mine.

Monday, December 23, 1985

Beautiful, sunny day; I'm off work today by taking an employment day that I didn't take earlier in the year. I'll also be off tomorrow (Christmas Eve) and Christmas Day. They're forecasting snow flurries for Christmas, and I'm looking forward to it. Maybe I'm seeking some excitement to this depressing and desolate period in my life.

Raymond is to get radiation treatment today at 4:00 p.m. after verifying this with the hospital. I told him that I'd like to go with him and ask the doctor some questions. He agreed that I could go. He doesn't look like he feels well. His eyes are puffy looking and he's thin after losing weight. He ate scrambled eggs, sausage, and toast for breakfast. After breakfast, he ate three tangerines.

Tuesday, December 24, 1985

I was awakened by the doorbell this morning. Sally, my friend and ex-co-worker, dropped by with a gift for me. It was a nice little "what not" that I put on the foyer table, and will cherish it. After getting up, I stayed up and started cooking breakfast, afterwards dinner, and potatoes for pies, etc.

Raymond got up, ate breakfast, and sat on the basement couch, arising only to put another log in the fireplace occasionally. By day's end, I had finished cooking two sweet potato pies, a chocolate cake, a ham and turkey. I also went out and bought a coconut cake.

Chapter Four

POST-HOLIDAY CELEBRATION; BEGINNING OF NEW YEAR AND OCCURRENCES OF NEW FEW MONTHS

Wednesday, December 25, 1985

At 12:50 a.m., Raymond is still sitting on the end of the couch looking at TV some, and listening to Christmas carols. It seems that he hates to turn loose Christmas Eve, and already it's Christmas Day. A few snow flurries fell Christmas Eve, and I'm hoping for more today.

My relatives are to meet at Bernard's house at 2:00 p.m. and exchange gifts. My heart goes out to Raymond with pity and wonder. Is this his last Christmas? If so, please Lord, help me to make it a good one for him, I pray. He has already cut a large piece of the chocolate cake, and is eating greedily, but remarking about the dryness of the cake, but it's good taste.

Kevron is in bed, still hoping Christmas Eve is like it used to be when he believed strongly in Santa Claus. At age 13 years, he still has doubts about this seemingly.

The telephone started ringing shortly after 7:30 a.m. The first call was from Eddie, Raymond's brother, wishing Raymond and us well. We had already been up and ate biscuits, ham, and coffee. Secondly, Nedra, Raymond's niece, called. Her mother, Alvis, Raymond's sister, also talked. We had been downstairs already and opened gifts which included a microwave oven for me. Raymond received a watch and a card that sings when opened. Ray, Jr. received pajamas, a $50 bill, and speakers for his component set. Juan received the same.

Kevron was enthused with his Colecovision set. Our sons pooled their money and bought us microwave dishes, an am/fm radio, small hair dryer and curler set for me, and a travel kit with cosmetics for their daddy. At 2:00 p.m. we were at Bernard's house, and many other gifts were received and given. Raymond and I received another am/fm radio with a cassette player, and a fern stand. I received a nice dress and perfume. Raymond received another nice cosmetic set. Kevron received an airplane that flies. Ray, Jr. and Juan received nice watches. Raymond held up well, but appears weak and puny; but, he smiled continuously, almost phony-like.

He was clean shaven and neatly dressed. He received a compliment on his shoes that are new and cost $80.

When we returned home, we ate heartily. We had a quiet evening, and Raymond retired early using for an excuse Kevron's playing with the Colecovision, cutting off his TV watching.

At 10:00 p.m., I awoke Raymond to see if he had gotten all of his medication taken for the day, and he said, "no." So, I bought the last pill to the bed. He informed me, he is to return to work tomorrow evening, and receive radiation treatments in the morning now at 8:00 a.m. He is to be at work at 3:00 p.m. He waits until the last minute to discuss these things with me. He has never wanted to worry me.

Ray, Jr. is to travel to Sommerville, Tennessee, tomorrow to be with his girlfriend, whose father has died. He is to be funeralized Friday. Ray will give her a Christmas present at this time. Raymond, Sr. gave him permission to rent a car for this trip. Ray, Jr. traveled successfully, and mentioned how sweetly his girlfriend sang a solo at her father's services.

Thursday, December 26, 1985

I worked at the hospital from 8:00 a.m. until 4:30 p.m. Raymond had a radiation treatment, and worked 3:00 p.m. until 11:30 p.m. He came home in an amorous mood. The weather was very cold, so was his skin. I was very tired and was sleeping when he came in. He tried to force his attention on me. With me pleading: "Stop, go on I'm tired and I don't want to do anything that might hurt you." After a near battle, he gave up, after many accusations as to "why you don't want me."

Friday, December 27, 1985

At 6:00 a.m., the alarm clock went off for me to get up. I felt guilty and sorry for not responding to poor Raymond last night. I told him I was ready for lovemaking and he did a good job to his and my surprise, I think. He has to be at the hospital at 8:00 a.m. for radiation therapy, so I warmed his car and mine. He will be driving Juan's car since his thermostat isn't working. Raymond's station wagon is parked behind Juan's car so, I didn't pull the cars out of the garage before starting them up to be warmed.

While at the hospital, Raymond thought about the possibility of carbon monoxide having escaped into the house, became frantic and called home. The children were asleep and didn't answer the phone. He rushed home to find Kevron with a headache, and Juan sleeping soundly. He believed it was due to the car fumes, and he was very upset. He told me, "If those children had died, you would never have been any more good." I agreed with him, and told him that I would have given up, been institutionalized. I really don't believe fumes had anything to do with these occurrences since the garage door was up.

Saturday, December 28, 1985

At 9:00 a.m., I awoke and started thinking about all of the duties of today--finding a beautician to do my hair since Al, Raymond's brother, is on vacation, and exchanging Bernard's Christmas gift. He is the one in the family with a Ph.D. degree, his wife works, he has no children, so we always ask him what he needs. My sister had communicated erroneously that he needed flatware. I bought flatware, but exchanged it for a cutlery set that he wanted. This is our wedding anniversary, so Raymond and I are going out to eat.

At 3:30 p.m., Raymond gets a call from his job inquiring as to why he isn't at work. He thought he was off, but no actual schedule is posted. Raymond doesn't normally drink anything alcoholic during the day, especially since he is taking medication, but today he drank two beers. So, in his hurry to dress for work, I insisted he brush his teeth, use mouthwash, and mints to disguise alcohol on his breath. I also warned him of a possible manipulation on the job--trying to get him to retire or go on disability. I later stopped by the sheet mill to see if he ate supper, and he had eaten a hamburger, french fries, and a drink. So, I came home to prepare for church tomorrow.

Sunday, December 29, 1985

I dressed for church, wearing the dress my sister from California sent me for Christmas. After hearing many testimonials about the goodness of God, listening to a guest soloist, and the sermon, we were home by 2:00 p.m. Today is Raymond's birthday. He is 54 years old today. He admonished me for not getting him a gift.

Our anniversary, his birthday, and Christmas have always been situated so gifts were not given for all occasions. I tried to cheer him up by teasing him about the possibility of his marrying a rich girl the next time.

Monday, December 30, 1985

At 6:00 a.m., the alarm goes off. Raymond is in an amorous mood again. I told him to ask his doctor's advice about sex, but he persists and I gave in. Later in the day, he urinated and found blood coming from his penis. So, I remarked, "I told you about so much sex--I give up." He then said to me, "That is something to tell your sick husband." He is still working evenings, so Ray, Jr. took him his meal of hot chili and cornbread, and a large Coke. Ray, Jr. also picked up his medicine from the drugstore and took it to him--Macrodantin, a drug for urinary tract problems. Later, Raymond told me that he's only had sex with me, and if he has some venereal disease, I'd better pack my bags.

I don't believe he's thought about the possibility of radiation reactions, metastasis, etc. But, I have. I pray, "Oh Lord, have mercy, give me the strength to hold out." I dread to look at him when he comes home from work. But since the radiation treatments have started, he is looking some better; he's eating better and gaining weight. Now, this bleeding--what can I expect next? The year 1986 promises to be something if any of us lives to see it. At 11:30 p.m., Raymond is home, seemingly feeling better. Today was payday, and he was paid $180. Somehow, his sick pay didn't come through. He doesn't seem worried about this, but I know that he is. With three sons, two in college, house bills, I know he is concerned. For this he is filing a "grievance" at U.S. Steel, a procedure followed by union-eligible employees. This is to obtain his other pay.

Tuesday, December 31, 1985

Raymond worked, came in and went to bed. No shooting of guns and the usual "pomp and circumstances" of New Years Eve. When 12:00 midnight came, I fell on my knees and prayed for upcoming 1986 events. I asked for strength.

Wednesday, January 1, 1986

Raymond, the children and I are at home today. I washed clothes, cooked a dinner of black-eyed peas, turnip greens, liver, pigs feet, and a cake. The football bowl games are on TV most of the day after the morning parades. Tomorrow we plan to take a family portrait. I'll have to leave work early, for the appointment is at 4:00 p.m. at Pizitz.

Thursday, January 2, 1986

My boss is back from vacation today. I'm glad. She has a way of holding the place in line. She is agreeable to letting me off early for the making of the portrait. All went well, except Juan, my second son, was dressed in a sweater and sport coat with no tie. Everyone else was fully dressed, including ties. Raymond went without urging or reluctance. In the past, he'd put up a fight.

Friday, January 3, 1986

Work for me was as usual, in ElderCare at Lloyd Noland Hospital. This ElderCare is a program for the elderly where no deductibles are necessary to be paid, no filing of claims, and no bills sent to the home. With a supplemental insurance (approved), Medicare and $30 a year, the clients are free to receive medical care and hospitalization. Of course, a program of educational seminars, exercise programs, and social events go along with being a member if one desires to partake of such activities. After work, I came home, cooked fried chicken livers, large lima beans cooked in the slow cooker while I worked, and cornbread. We drank cola and ate leftover cake. I sent Raymond his dinner. He had a radiation treatment today.

Saturday, January 4, 1986

Barbara Gail, my sister, called after 10:00 a.m. She, Kevron, and I are to return the Colecovision he received at Christmas because it malfunctions. None are in stock, so he received the money. Afterwards we rode around in Pratt City, my hometown. But the area we toured was Westchester, somewhat of a suburb. Many nice homes are there, but so many are vacant, seemingly repossessed. I thought in my mind, it must be a sign of the times and economic pressures.

Ray, Jr. and Juan left for school in Tennessee before I left home. Ray, Jr. seemed so anxious to return to school. I cautioned him about rushing on the highway. I'm always tense and "uneasy" until I know they have reached their destination. Seemingly, they can't understand this, or don't think about it. It'll be when they are parents before they really understand, I'm sure.

My sister gave me $100 of the money awarded her after she received the wrong medications by phone order to a druggist here in the City. She settled out-of-court, got only a small amount, but the lawyers didn't think she had a strong case. Some of her medical problems were pre-existing, and the M.D. that called the prescription in had a heavy accent. So, we went out to eat after shopping with the money she gave me. She wanted me to buy clothes for myself and not spend it on house furnishings, like I have a tendency to do. On the way back home, we stopped and got Raymond a bar-b-cue sandwich, and took it to U.S. Steel. The doctors had told him to eat more and he is trying seemingly. All in all, I had a day away from home, which is rare for me, and I feel better.

Sunday, January 5, 1986

I got up before 9:00 a.m. and cooked a quick meal in the microwave oven, or tried to anyway. I was through in 10 minutes, using the conventional stove to brown the biscuits, and scramble the eggs. Raymond went back to bed after eating. He got up around 10:00 a.m. and went to church, taking his clothes that he wears at work with him. He asked me to bring lunch to him after church, and I did. The meal consisted of broccoli, fried corn, American potatoes, and cubed steak and gravy. I bought a cake, along with peaches, for dessert.

As I listened to my church broadcast on the radio, I cooked this meal. Later, I went to the laundromat and dried clothes because the washer at home works fine, but the dryer is broken. As I came from the laundromat, Raymond was on the telephone requesting his meal by 5:00 p.m., along with an antacid. He was also disturbed because he couldn't find his iron tablets before leaving home. I found the iron medication, Mylanta, and took it as I carried the food. When I arrived at his workplace, I found him with what he called "severe gas," and not looking well. If I had known, I would have been there earlier.

When I returned home, Kevron was watching TV. He has a 10-page typed report due Wednesday at school, and he hasn't written it. He was reprimanded, and I called Bernard to do the typing with my apologies. He, as usual, assured me he is happy to do it. Later, he told me "not to be so hard on the boy." I wonder to myself, "Oh Lord, which way should I turn?" as my paternal grandmother used to say. "If it ain't one thing, it's two; if it ain't two, it's 22."

† The Cross And Weeping Still †

Monday, January 6, 1986

This is Raymond's last day for radiation therapy. Today at work, it was hectic for me. Before I cooked supper, I proofread Kevron's report that's due Wednesday, making corrections so it can be typed. Then I cooked homemade soup, fixed hot dogs and kraut, and Kool-Aid as a drink. Then off to U.S. Steel.

Raymond and I had eaten donuts and oranges. His appetite isn't so good now, I didn't think he'd eat much. He did eat the wiener and kraut, but didn't eat the soup. He asked that the crackers and Kool-Aid be left so that he could eat later.

While at his workplace, a truck came and waited for Raymond to take some papers as protocol dictated. Raymond walked so slowly to the truck. I remarked to Kevron, "He shouldn't be working." Kevron immediately said, "Don't say that to him, ma." Poor thing (Raymond) continues to push himself. Later, a lady called to say her heat went off, and she needs Raymond to fix it. I wanted to tell her, "He is sick," but I wouldn't. I took the telephone number and I'll let him handle it as he desires. You see, he does air conditioning/refrigeration along with working at U.S. Steel for a living.

Saturday, January 11, 1986

Got out of bed before 9:00 a.m. I consider this late, but since working all week, I rested some this morning. I do have a full day ahead, with grocery shopping, drying clothes after they're washed, cleaning house, and going to the beauty shop. Later in the day, I stopped at Raymond's place of employment, as if by compulsion. I just wanted to see if he needed anything. When I arrived, he was eating lima beans, rice, and smothered chicken that I had fixed at home this morning. He had used a hot plate and boiler to heat it. His appetite is better, and he is looking better.

Last night I dreamed of a funeral. I don't know whose funeral, but what stands out in my mind were some red and white flowers. The white ones were the whitest flowers I have ever seen.

Before Raymond went to work, a Jehovah Witness came by and had a "lesson" and prayer with Raymond. This man comes by weekly. I wonder if he knows how sick Raymond is. Last week he made a remark to Raymond about weight loss. If I ever see him away from Raymond, I think I'll tell him so he'll know better how to deal and talk with my husband. Yesterday I got paid, so I sent the boys $100. Raymond is buying their books for the semester.

Tuesday, January 14, 1986

Raymond is working the 11:00 p.m. to 7:00 a.m. shift, and I feel out of control. I can't watch him as well. He isn't eating the hot meals I prepare. He complained of gas pains earlier, and took some sodium bicarbonate to relieve it. I checked on him several times to see if the pain is worsening, apparently it isn't. You see, I'm at work during the day, and he's at work during the night. As he prepared to leave for work, he took the back brace with him. I believe his back is hurting again. He doesn't discuss himself very openly.

Oh, can I go through bathing him, lifting him out of bed, dressing him, sitting him in a chair before leaving for work again? That's what happened before the first radiation treatments, and it took two weeks of treatment before he got relief from the back pain. I'm worried and I'm scared. If his back starts hurting so badly again, what now?

Monday, January 20, 1986

I'm upset today on a whole. Celebrating Dr. Martin Luther King's birthday arouses me. I had known Dr. King when I was a young woman studying nursing in Atlanta, Georgia, in the 1960's. His birthday is a national holiday, but the school my youngest son now attends convenes anyway. But Kevron didn't want to go, and we didn't make him. Raymond and he went downtown to a park to see the unveiling of Dr. King's statue, erected in his honor.

Another reason I'm upset is that I found the poinsettia bought by my sister, Gail, to be put on Mama's grave couldn't be put down. As Robert, Gail's husband, went to put it on the grave, he couldn't find the marker. Seemingly, a burial took place near Mama's grave, and it was disturbed--even the marker. I alerted both brothers, Leon and Bernard. The latter called me this evening and assured me by tomorrow, even a minor crookedness of the tombstones would be straightened out. I plan to by a plot right next to her, to be used by any family member.

Now, my poor Raymond is cranky these days. He wears the back brace to work, he lifts his legs out of the car with his hands, and walks with a gait disturbance.

He has hired some men to trim trees so that grass will grow on the northwest side of the house next year. "It's too shady now," he says. We went to church yesterday and last Sunday. The planned sermon is a continuation "In the Meantime" for next Sunday, and I hope we'll be there. Raymond goes to bed when I come home from work, and he eats no vegetables. I'm so worried about him. The cold he's had for quite a while is about gone, and he didn't develop pneumonia.

Sunday, January 26, 1986

This is an overcast looking day. We were awakened by a truck being struck in the mud on the empty lot next to our home. Seemingly, there is preparation to build something there, which is disturbing to us. Probably a business will be next to us--a residential section. After the truck remained stuck, a man got out, got into a tractor, and pushed the truck out of the mud. I then asked Raymond if he planned to go to church today, and he said "Yes, I don't know when I may get down sick again." I assured him by saying, "None of us knows that." Then I asked him what he wanted for breakfast, and he said, "I don't know." I guess Satan arose in me and I proceeded to say, "You can't even tell me what you want, and when you come back from church, dinner will be done. I wish I were like that--maybe if I had a maid." He said, "If you had a Ph.D. degree, you could afford to hire a maid." I then said, "Jacqueline Kennedy or Mrs. Reagan doesn't have a Ph.D." He said, "They married the presidents." I said, "It depends on who you marry, doesn't it?" This ended the argument.

Now I'm wondering to myself, what made me say those things? I guess I sometimes get tired. As I prepared a breakfast of pancakes, link sausage, coffee, and orange juice, I thought, "How silly or out-of-place for me to start Sunday morning like this." I then called Gail, my sister, who is sick with the flu, and was treated at a local emergency room Friday. She teaches school, and was glad to hear of the weather forecast and a possibility of being out of school due to snow tomorrow. Her son, Brian, was hyperactive last night and she got little sleep. I encouraged her to listen to my minister on the radio today. His message is to deal with overcoming grief, but she said she is going back to sleep. Oh, how I'm praying for her. She has still not dealt with Mama's death well.

Monday, January 27, 1986

With an unshaven face, ashen color, and slow gait, Raymond leaves for work (at 9:00 p.m.). I reminded him to fasten his shirt sleeves. I also asked him about his tie that he is not wearing, and is a part of his uniform. He has told me many times in the past that he hates ties because his mother made him wear them to school when he was a boy. So, he goes off to work. He worked last night, and was up shortly after noon working on a job at Christian Industrial Hall in Fairfield, installing some kind of motor.

He came home and rigged up a light to keep the water line from freezing in this frigid weather we're experiencing. He later ate a bowl of soup and talked about how good it was.

He then went to bed, but shortly afterwards I heard him up in the kitchen. He was taking sodium bicarbonate for gas. He is slowing down for sure. I'm so concerned and worried. I informed him of the pneumonia vaccine available, one shot only. He doesn't appear at all enthusiastic about it.

Last night I had a weird dream. In it I saw a book, seemingly a wooden one, white with red flowers on top called "THE CROSS." Seemingly a play was being cast from this book, and I saw people I've never known. The leading man got away before I could contact him for his part, so I suggested my brother, Bernard, could probably do the part. The dream has haunted me most of the day!

Anyway, maybe Raymond will shave at work as he often does. I ask myself, "What am I to do with two boys in college, a sick husband, and a 13-year old son that's overweight?

Wednesday, January 29, 1986

I worked hard today at work. I sent two patients to the doctor directly because of severe medical problems. Usually, I see them, make an appointment for a doctor's visit later, after a nursing assessment is done. But, after work, Raymond met me at the studio to pick out what pictures would be included in the family portrait. The pictures were beautiful. Earlier today, Raymond saw the radiologist who reassured him, and told him to keep taking his medications. He said, "It'll take time for the radiation treatments to be effective." I can see he isn't as strong as he has been. He walks in a stooped manner, and seemingly, painfully. However, he's elated over having gained four pounds since his last doctor's visit.

Tuesday, February 4, 1986

Raymond's working 11:00 p.m. to 7:00 a.m. has me baffled. I wonder if working this shift is causing problems, or if he's going "downhill fast." His right leg and foot are swollen, he has gas pains and is taking Mylanta and sodium bicarbonate regularly. I warned him about taking too much soda and possibly getting his blood electrolytes out of balance. He struggles on to work, taking his shaving equipment with him in order to shave. He seems to sense some impending illness.

He had the trees cut down and limbs cut off, and he's having a hole dug for the waste to run in another direction from the cesspool. He warned us yesterday to have Kevron's cosmetic breast surgery done while he's still working. (Kevron is obese and has excess mammary gland tissue.) He had exterminators come and spray for roaches--all in preparation for something it seems. I worry and pray for him. He is cranky at times, but still so precious. Kevron follows him to the door each night, and worries that he is working too hard. He tries to get me to have his daddy to report off work, but he won't do it. Where is this leading us? I pray so hard--"Oh Lord, help me."

Monday, February 10, 1986

The feelings, I have tonight, I must express. Raymond is in bed after taking sodium bicarbonate and Mylanta. He complains of gas and his right leg hurting. I've tried to get him to take a strong pain pill, but he refuses. He takes only Bufferin. He refers to his leg pain as arthritis. Now he's working a "swing" shift. This morning I was up at 4:30 a.m. to fix his breakfast, before he left for work. He ate leftover roast beef and rice for breakfast. He seems to be going downhill so fast. I'm helpless in helping him it seems. I've always been considered a good nurse, and I've helped countless others. There is a procedure performed on surgical patients now, allowing them to push the gas through the intestine in a methodical manner. I'll bring the article home for him to read.

As he sleeps, he looks like a dying person. I've been told by some of my colleagues that Raymond should express himself on death and dying—things he wants done or not done--but he never engages in this kind of conversation. Maybe, he will come to it. I don't want to do anything to add to his suffering or hasten his death. I've worked today and must retire so I can get up with him at 4:30 a.m. and prepare breakfast. I returned to bed a short while before getting out to work myself.

Wednesday, February 12, 1986 (7:30 a.m.)

Raymond informed me that he is now about to go to the University of Alabama in Birmingham (UAB) doctors. He feels that his present doctors aren't doing enough for him. His gas is now gone since he started taking an herbal laxative pill nightly. His brother, Al, gave them to him. I was preparing to go to work when he told me of the doctor change, and somehow, this disturbed me all day.

I asked myself, "Why change?" Is he feeling worse? He looks better! Will the new doctors perform some new experiment on him? That night he called home before getting off from work. He was working 3:00 p.m. to 11:00 p.m. shift. I asked if I could go to the doctor with him next Friday, and he said, "No, you'll talk too much." Now, I'm wondering if he will hold back needed information about himself. I worked Saturday to have an extra day that I can take as off time. This would be ideal so that I can go along with him to the new doctors. Is Raymond experiencing a form of denial; yet, reaching out for further help?

Saturday, February 15, 1986

Yesterday was Valentines Day. We had a Valentines party at work for the elderly. I bought Raymond and Kevron a card and a box of candy. Raymond gave me a card, as I'm on a diet. He usually gives me candy, however. Today, Raymond left home at 10:00 a.m. to do some refrigeration work at a store in Fairfield that's being refurbished. The man that usually gives him a weekly lesson (Jehovah Witness) came by after Raymond was gone. Raymond left word for him that he had tried unsuccessfully to contact him, thus cancelling the lesson. This gave me the opportunity to mention to the gentleman Raymond's ailment. I told him that Raymond had cancer--the shock in his eyes almost made me sorry that I mentioned it. He had tears in his eyes. I believe now he can "witness" to Raymond in another way, with emphasis upon salvation. He will also know not to mention things like weight loss to him.

I worked as usual today--washing, cleaning, and getting ready for work next week. I was nervous and tense, and dreaded seeing Raymond come home from work moving very stiffly. We had planned to go to see the movie, "The Color Purple" this afternoon. So I went to get grocery after Raymond returned, hoping to be home by 4:00 p.m. But, instead, the lights went out at the store, delaying me. We needed gas in the car, and it was 5:00 p.m. before we arrived at the movies, thus we had missed the first and most important part of the movie. It showed only once. Later Raymond made a remark that tension made me go off to the grocery store, knowing that we should have been going to the movies. You know, he was right. At times, especially on weekends, I'm at a loss: confused, worried, sometimes hostile, and try to stay busy.

Friday night was Kevron's Boy Scout Banquet. The theme was "It's better to build a boy than to mend a man." The food was delicious. Raymond made remarks all the way home about the greens that were served. He said that they tasted like those his mama used to cook. I told him, "The cook didn't work." He talked about that not having anything to do with it. Kevron then started by saying, "Auntie Gail works, and she's a good cook. Mama is a good cook too, but sometimes she throws things together." I, being hurt, came back with, "My sisters and brothers say that I cook more than anyone that they've ever seen." This quieted the conversation, and the mood of the festivities was somewhat ruined. I thought quietly--"A man never changes, cancer or not."

Sunday, February 23, 1986

Raymond was having trouble with his neck being stiff now. I learned through Kevron that Raymond fell recently while working on an air conditioning job. I attribute his neck discomfort to this, but I don't know. Last Friday (February 21, 1986), he went to an oncologist at UAB. The doctor viewed Raymond's previous records and made a follow-up appointment for one month. The new doctor drew blood for laboratory studies, and told Raymond a CAT scan and X-rays will have to be done. Raymond seemed depressed after his visit, looking blankly into space.

Saturday, his day off from his regular job was spent putting a walk-in cooler in a store. Sunday, he worked from 6:00 a.m. to 3:30 p.m. at U.S. Steel, then went directly back to the store where he was Saturday. He is to help the electrician "tie in" the walk-in cooler to electrical power. I went to church where I grew up, Metropolitan C.M.E., Ensley, Alabama, to hear the minister in concert. He sang to help raise money for the church, I am told. I saw aunts, uncles, and cousins while there. You see, this is a small family-oriented church. After I returned, and before retiring, I advised Raymond to take a warm shower, and I rubbed him with Ben Gay. This, along with taking pain medication orally, seems to make him rest better. He still grunts when getting into our bed.

Yesterday, I told his brother Al (my hair stylist) what Dr. Moon had said about Raymond's life expectancy. He was visibly shaken, and to my surprise asked, "What kind of cancer has he?"

Thursday, February 27, 1986

Raymond came home from work looking tired and weak. He had a grayish color to his skin. I assisted him with getting his coat off, and he blurted out, "I'm tired of hurting, I'm so tired of hurting I don't know what to do." This was his first outburst since being sick.

Monday, March 3, 1986

Raymond had to be at work at 5:00 a.m. He was up at 4:00 a.m. I stayed in bed, and took his breakfast and lunch by the job as I went to work. When I got home from work, the men had finished sanding and varnishing three hardwood floors upstairs. I was surprised because they didn't shine much. They advised me to put paste wax on them and buff them. Maybe when Ray, Jr. and Juan come back from college, they can help with that during A.E.A. Week. Raymond has the facial expression of someone in pain, but refuses to take prescription medication to alleviate it. He takes extra strength Bufferin. This disturbs Kevron, almost to the point of tears. Raymond denies pain, but had Kevron put a heat lamp to his shoulder for what he calls bursitis. He is very cranky and irritable these days. I'm sure it's a combination of pain and generally not feeling well. Also, a friend and former co-worker called Raymond, and they talked about the possibility of Raymond's job being abolished at U.S. Steel. This, along with his other problems, worries him. He would rather do anything than not work, seemingly. Kevron is trying to get him to go back to church to a healing ceremony, and I agreed. He told us to leave him alone. I told him that he doesn't want to be healed, and that he's tired. He denied it. All of this is beginning to wear on my nerves. I look tired, feel tired, and plan to take a week vacation starting next week. I'm thinking that I may need to save this time for later, however. Raymond doesn't look good.

Thursday, March 6, 1986

Kevron, the youngest son, was told about his daddy's cancer today. As we traveled to take Raymond's supper to work, he reminded me that he knew why his daddy's arm hurt. "He keeps his window down when he drives. I've told him not to do it, but he won't listen." As I drove, I told him, "Darling, your daddy has a disease, that's why his arm hurts." He asked, "What kind of disease?" I said, "I'd rather not discuss it." He said, "Mama, you've said that much, now what kind of disease?" I said, "Cancer, son."

He was stunned. He seemingly wanted to cry, but didn't. After we got to where Raymond was, Kevron wouldn't talk. He acted like he was angry and pouting. As we drove home, he said, "Mama, I didn't know it would be cancer," and he sobbed and cried. I patted him on the leg and said, "Let it out, son, cry if you want. I've cried and cried." I warned him not to discuss this with his daddy now, however.

Friday, March 7, 1986

Ray, Jr. and Juan came home for spring break, bringing three friends of Juan--supper for eight and breakfast for eight. Then, Juan and his friends were off to Fort Walton Beach, Florida. Ray, Jr. stayed back here with us.

Saturday March 9, 1986

As I was mopping the floor, I turned awkwardly, heard my back pop, and pain set in. This has happened before.

Sunday, March 10, 1986

I went to church. Near the end of the sermon I thought about the oven being on low heat cooking chicken, and I forgot and left the cornbread in the lower oven. After church, I felt cold and terrible. I called my younger sister, Gail, and mentioned it to her. In a few hours she came over with antibiotics that really helped me. Seemingly, the Lord wants me to rest. This is the beginning of my vacation, and I am sick. I don't feel like doing a lot of cleaning and etc. So, I'm resting. This is something I rarely do.

Saturday, March 16, 1986

The spring vacation period is about over. Ray, Jr. is preparing to go back to Tennessee State University in Nashville, Tennessee. Juan is still in Fort Walton Beach, Florida. He did arrive about 7:00 p.m. with his three friends that he traveled with. They ate collard greens, creamed white potatoes, ham, lime pie, and cornbread. They also drank tea. I saw Raymond, Sr. talking harshly to Juan several times, seemingly upset.

After Juan was gone, I confronted Raymond with why. What had Juan done? What he told me was one of the most astonishing, traumatic occurrences I've been associated with. Juan had nearly drowned while in Florida, had been in the hospital's intensive care unit for two days. He had been swept out in the ocean by waves. When I learned this, Juan was already gone back to school. His friends, Raymond, and Juan had concealed this, hoping I wouldn't find out. I had a sick husband and other stresses, they thought. I didn't need another. When they arrived at school, they called back, and I told Juan that I knew of his ordeal. He mentioned that God had spoken to him as he had given up to die, "Do you want to live, or do you want to die?" Juan said that it seemed easier to die, but he thought about us and how we loved him, and said, "Live." At that time, someone got him by the neck and pulled him ashore, placed him on his stomach, and he vomited. He received resuscitation that saved his life.

I've been told that his nail beds and skin color was purple as he was rushed to Humana Hospital. Several news articles were printed about the incident. Afterwards, I wrote the newspaper with words of thanks to the unknown rescuers. Later an article was sent to me. A high school student, David, had received the Carnegie Medal and $2,500 for his heroism of saving my son, Juan, then 20 years old, from drowning. I prayed and thanked God for sparing Juan. I also encouraged him to give his life and soul to God. Juan says that he sees things in a "different light" than before.

Monday, March 17, 1986

I called the school dormitory to check on Juan's condition. He notes some dryness of lips, and dehydration. He is forcing fluids by mouth.

Tuesday, March 18, 1986

I called the school to check on Juan, and he sounds very depressed. He said that he is studying. I feel depressed also. Later, I received a call from my first cousin, Annette, telling me that her dad, my Uncle Booker, has had a heart attack and is hospitalized. I notified my sisters and brothers, uncles, and aunts.

Friday, March 21, 1986

Uncle Booker had emergency bypass surgery today. My uncle from Chicago and aunts from Mississippi are coming to see about their brother. Uncle Quinton, from Chicago, Illinois, and two of his children are to live with me while here. They are to leave Sunday.

Wednesday, March 26, 1986

Raymond is having a lot of leg pains. He suffers so much sometimes. After I gave him two Empirin #3 tablets, an Advil, and a muscle relaxant, he got some relief, seemingly.

Thursday, March 27, 1986

Raymond and I walked to Hueytown Plaza to a nearby car dealership and looked at a new car. We leisurely walked back home. As we walked I wondered, "How long is this going to last?" Today he looks fairly well, and I love him so much. After returning from the walk, Raymond ate fairly well. He is sleeping well as I write this note.

Friday, April 4, 1986

Earlier this week I dreamed that my parental cousin, Prentice, is pregnant. She looked so big, like she was ready to deliver, but seemingly someone said that she has two months to go. Now she is beyond childbearing age. My parents always said that if you dream about a woman, it's concerning a man, and vice versa. I wonder if this dream has any significance in my life.

Yesterday, Raymond was off work and put some new ceiling tiles up in the basement. When I got home from work he looked tired and sick. However, we managed to go shopping for Kevron some clothes that he badly needed. We were to leave and shop before the first store closed at 5:00 p.m. No matter how Raymond tried, he couldn't get ready to go. So, I told him we'd come back for him later, and finish shopping at some stores that stayed open late. When we got into the car, Raymond asked Kevron to raise the neck rest up so he could lean back as we drove. People in the store stared at him because he looked so sick, leaning on the counters.

I had called home earlier today to check on him. He ate leftover peas for lunch, and he wanted croaker fish for supper. So, I cooked it, along with spaghetti. He declined his oatmeal cake for dessert, and asked that it be put in his lunch. He is having some trouble passing his urine. Yesterday he went to the drugstore and bought Azo-Standard (an over-the-counter medication) to aid in his urinary difficulties. His urinary flow has slowed down. I advised him to go and see the oncologist. I fear further metastasis. He remained in bed, and went to work at 9:40 p.m. Overall, he tries to act normal, but is somewhat grouchy. He walks with his right shoulder raised. His right leg is swollen. His height is diminishing, and a hump in his back is now prominent.

Friday, April 11, 1986

To see Raymond, a poor bent over figure, with a slow gait, going to work is pitiful. He overslept Wednesday, when he should have been at work by 1:00 p.m. His co-workers and boss wondered how he could sleep too late during the day. Anyway, he went to the company doctor at their request. He bragged to me, "The doctor found nothing." Raymond is getting tired now, though. He was off Thursday, and went to the Social Security office to inquire about retiring.

'He found out that one cannot retire while working. He plans to take off the next two weeks sick, and proceed with securing disability benefits. He is so pitiful looking to me. I worked hard at work today, but came home to take Kevron to the Boy Scouts meeting. I came back home to cook fresh vegetable soup, and to wash and clean the house that looks awful. Believe me, Raymond isn't physically able to help me at all!

Sunday, April 13, 1986

Raymond, Kevron, and I went to church today. This is the first day of Raymond's period away from work. He seems to feel and look better already. He really shouldn't be working now!

Thursday, April 17, 1986

Raymond went to see an orthopedist today because of leg pains. He is seeking medical help to get on disability from work.

Friday, April 18, 1986

Raymond went to the largest hospital in the city today, visiting the oncologist. There his pain medication was changed to Tylox instead of Darvocet N. It is also to be taken orally. The oncologist promised to write a letter to the Social Security Department to get disability benefits started. The oncologist also prescribed a new medication to be given by injection, called Leupron. This medication, hopefully, will decrease cancer activity. His hemoglobin, or blood count, is 7, which is low. (Normal is 14-18 Gm.) There is mention of a blood transfusion if the new medication doesn't increase his blood count. The medication had to be ordered by the pharmacist, and is very expensive. Ray, Jr. and Juan came home to surprise us for the weekend.

Tuesday, April 22, 1986

The Leupron came, and the first injection--0.2 cc was given by me. That night Raymond walked the floor, and sat up in bed complaining of "hot flashes" when questioned about why he was up so much. He never voluntarily complains of anything.

Saturday, April 26, 1986

After cleaning the house, Raymond, Kevron, and I set out in the car to do many errands. First, to a Fairfield grocery store to collect money for air conditioning work he had done there. Secondly, to the bank, the gas station, and later to Bernard's, my brother's, home. We then got grocery and dropped back by the Dairy Queen to get footlong hot dogs, milk shakes, and a sundae for me. My sister, Gail, and her son, Brian, came over later. She bought me some outfits to wear to work. She is so generous.

Sunday, April 27, 1986

Today at church a Women's Day celebration is in process. This is a money-raising event, more fanfare than religion. My sister, Gail, mentioned on yesterday how tired I looked. Raymond's iron medication has caused constipation, so he has taken a laxative. So, I doubt if I'll go to church. Also, Raymond was up during the night putting on a back brace, changing underclothes after accidents, and just sitting on the side of the bed seeking relief, seemingly. This is the first time that I've begun to wonder how long my wonderful, merciful God is going to let Raymond suffer. He stares blankly into space, appears scared, worried, and depressed at times. He is looking forward to the boys coming home next weekend. He wants them to get into his air conditioning business, but I hope the boys will work 9:00 a.m. to 5:00 p.m. jobs doing something else.

Tuesday, April 30, 1986

Today was hectic at work for me. I was extremely tense. When I got home, Raymond was very weak looking, and needed to shave, and also was irritable, somewhat. He did eat a good supper. We discussed our hospital coverage, and there is a question of our having family coverage after looking at the hospital cards. Raymond mentions wanting to by a Cadillac, but believe me, I don't know where the money is coming from. Yesterday, Raymond went to see a urologist. The doctor assured me that he thought the urinary tract infection had cleared since Raymond had completed his treatment of Bactrim DS for it. Raymond felt weak after returning home, and called the oncologist, who is at another hospital from the urologist. The doctor he called was nice, and mentioned that he could come in for treatment at any time necessary. He is to see the oncologist Friday, and I'll go with him. I hope he will be transfused. Maybe his appetite and overall health will improve.

Friday, May 2, 1986

I stayed off from work today. I took it as overtime due me since I worked on a Saturday at a shopping mall. The purpose of being off was to take Raymond in for a blood transfusion. His appointment time is 2:00 p.m. Now, I'm thinking, "It's awfully late to start a transfusion at this hour." But, this is what Raymond said, so I went on. After he saw the doctor, he was tested or typed and cross-matched so he could be given three units of blood (packed red cells) Monday. The children are here from school and can take him--luckily for me. It's hard to keep getting off from work. However, one does what has to be done.

Before getting to the hospital, I had errands to run: first, I went to get my payroll check, only to find that it had been picked up and taken to ElderCare, in, in the clinic where I work. Raymond was out n the car. We left and went to the bank, where the lines were long. Everyone is being paid, it seems, especially Social Security recipients. I needed gas in the car and rushed on after filling the tank. We made it to the oncology clinic by 1:45 p.m. The parking deck was nearly full, but, we found a place on the fifth and final deck.

Saturday, May 3, 1986

Today, I had to work from 10:00 a.m. to 2:00 p.m. at ElderCare's Open House. There was a fair response to the affair. Later, Kevron and I went to the hair care shop. When I got home, I found Raymond dribbling urine, and his clothes were wet. I thought, "He is becoming incontinent (unable to control his urine)." Thank God, I know something about medicine. I called around and found a place that sells condoms and leg bags, allowing the urine to have a receptacle to flow in, preventing wetness.

I took Raymond to the Emergency Room, where a urinalysis was done revealing 1 to 2 white blood cells, but a prescription for 40 Macrodantin was issued. Raymond has been very depressed since the visit to the oncologist on yesterday. I don't know if it's the idea of getting blood, or seeing the other oncology patients. He even called his sister and told her how depressed he is. She later told me that she could hardly sleep that night, but she gave Raymond a lecture on not being depressed--she said, "This isn't the time." I'm going to talk to the urologist on Monday. Raymond will also talk to the oncologist about this incontinence (inability to hold his urine). I'm thinking--"Lord, what's next?" My sons, who are home from school, will have to put off looking for a job tomorrow (and possibly Tuesday) to help their daddy, but I know that things will work out. I know they will.

Sunday, May 4, 1986

We didn't go to church. Raymond appears relaxed with his condom catheter and leg bag intact. This prevents him from being wet.

Monday, May 5, 1986

Raymond saw the oncologist, and was transfused with three units of packed red cells (blood). I talked with the urologist where I worked, and he agreed to see him at 11:00 a.m. tomorrow.

Chapter Five

HOSPITALIZATION OF RAYMOND (MAY) AND POST HOSPITALIZATION: 1986

Tuesday, May 6, 1986

Raymond saw the urologist and it was discovered that he needs to see a neurologist. He needs to have a myelogram test, and possibly, further radiation therapy. While I was at work, Raymond called me about 4:00 p.m., and said that he would have to be admitted to the hospital. He sounded sad, and I reassured him. I was allowed to come home 30 minutes early, get his pajamas, etc. and go over to the hospital. The doctors explained everything thoroughly.

Wednesday, May 7, 1986

The myelogram was scheduled for 1:00 p.m. Raymond had a breakfast of clear liquids. The preparation and test lasted about two and one-half hours. The results revealed metastasis to the spinal column, with further need of radiation. Formerly, a CT scan had been planned, but was cancelled after they found these results. The doctor, a black female, explained to him that paralysis could result if he didn't take the radiation required to reduce the tumor. She said that the tumor itself could cause paralysis. This troubled Raymond greatly. But, he refused to sign for radiation until further consultations were held. However, he had received one radiation treatment already. He kept the form to sign for other radiation treatments with him in the hospital, and agreed to bring it back signed later.

Juan got his driver's license renewed, and also a call from Kelly Services offering him a landscaping job for $4.00 plus an hour. Ray, Jr. is working on air conditioners for his daddy. Ray's girlfriend has a brother who is a minister. He said that the Lord came to him and advised him to come to Birmingham to pray. I wonder and hope this is the beginning of a miracle of complete healing. Somehow I can't accept what is happening. He (the minister) is coming from the airport and going directly to the hospital near midnight. I am so exhausted. I left the hospital about 9:00 p.m. to prepare the minister's bed. I bought fried chicken, juice, etc. on the way home. Raymond seems upset at my leaving the hospital, and I'd been there since 8:30 a.m. this morning. Oh Lord, I pray, pray, pray.

Sunday, May 11, 1986

Raymond remains hospitalized. This week has been stressful for him. The oncologist, neurologist, and neurosurgeon all disagree on the proper treatment at this time. X-rays of his spinal column showed diffuse metastasis. The complaint of pain in his left arm today prompted an x-ray which showed metastasis. Raymond is very edgy and nervous. He mentioned this to me, and I mentioned it to the doctor, upsetting Raymond. He told me, "I'm sorry I ever said anything about it." I also mentioned to the nurse that extra nourishments like milkshakes were not being sent, and Raymond again got upset.

He thinks that when I mention things like this, I am complaining. He doesn't want to "rock the boat." I know how things get mixed up in a large institution. My nursing experience has taught me this. I can see that Raymond needs a tranquilizer. One of the residents explained to me that a meeting of the minds will exist tomorrow, and they'll collectively decide what areas definitely are to be radiated, and if chemotherapy will be instilled at the time of a spinal tap that is to be done for cytology studies. This might help with controlling the urine. This whole matter is complicated and disturbing to us all. The final decision: radiation only!

The other night, Friday, I believe Raymond's sister took him for a walk down the hall while visiting the hospital. This left her husband and me alone. I mentioned to him that Raymond's brother had been exposed to too much heat during this hot weather, and couldn't come to the hospital.

My brother-in-law thinks all of this is "bull." I also mentioned his other brother hadn't visited or called recently. His brother, Al, called Saturday and said that he would visit Raymond on Sunday. I left the hospital at 8:30 p.m., and he still had not come. Since he does my hair, I've heard him mention sending flowers and visiting his patrons. I wonder why brothers brought up to be "close" behave in this manner. Is it the avoidance of unpleasant things? Tomorrow, I plan to go to work. Maybe my nerves and Raymond's will be better.

Friday, May 15, 1986

Raymond came home from the hospital yesterday. He was so glad to be home. He walked outside and seemingly communed with nature. I feel so exhausted from working and going to the hospital, and keeping up with things at home. He returned to the hospital for a radiation treatment today. The oncologist told him that he would radiate his hip also. Seemingly, he'll be going to the hospital daily for quite a while. At supper, each day, he tries to eat but grunts and grunts.

I was staring at him as he grunted, and he looked at me and asked, "Am I grunting too much?" He is so very pitiful. I ask in my heart, somewhat ashamed, "How much more?" Then I think, "The Lord isn't going to put any more on us than we can bear." Yesterday, he was able to eat prepared frozen lima beans; boiled chicken seasoned with sage, onions, and celery; fried okra; and iced tea. Today, he ate liver, rice and gravy, peas and carrots, and drank cola.

To add to our frustrations, Juan's grades came from Tennessee State University, and were horrible. I wonder if his father's illness is affecting him, or if his near brush with death prevented him from studying well. My co-workers are nice to me, and this helps. I look so worn and tired in the face. I guess I worry about this because I've always been known as being pretty.

Sunday, May 17, 1986

Raymond and I did not go to church today, but the boys did. We've almost had a drought recently, but today it is raining. Raymond came down the stairs to eat breakfast like a toddler, holding the rail, and taking each step carefully at a time. His shoulders are bony, and his skin is darker than usual. There is no radiation this weekend. He isn't having any nausea right now, but sometimes speaks of weakness, especially on the days that he gets radiation therapy. Now, this weekend, even this grunting has stopped. After the radiation treatments cease, maybe he can go back to church. I sent a donation of $10.00 and he sent $75.00 to church by the boys. Raymond's appetite is better today. He ate a roast pork sandwich before the boys could come back from church. After they got home, we all sat down and ate dinner. I served fresh string beans and white potatoes, tossed salad, roast pork, banana nut bread, white bread, and iced tea. Raymond spent most of the day sitting up in a chair, nodding at intervals.

Yesterday he followed Ray, Jr. as he fixed air conditioners. Seemingly, this helped his morale, gave him a sense of worth. He brought two cheap recliners back. They are low, non-sturdy recliners that cost $19.00 each. Seemingly, he is seeking comfort in any way he can find it. I suggested that he use the recliner in Juan's room. We didn't put it back upstairs after the hardwood floors were revarnished. It has a high back and is more comfortable than the low ones he bought.

At 9:00 p.m., he is in bed, but if he does as he did last night, he'll be up walking before long. He needs a nerve pill or sleeping pill so badly. He doesn't have one. When I mentioned this in the hospital, he became hysterical, so my hands are tied. If I mention a problem, Raymond seems to make it appear to be my problem. The doctors then pay less attention to the neurotic, complaining wife.

In trying to get up out of the chair, he needs help sometimes, and his left arm is so sore that he cannot hold the telephone well. His cousin, Ida, called today and talked only a short while. She probably became emotionally upset, and cried. Raymond wouldn't say. On a whole, his family members aren't as attentive as I think they should be. I don't understand the rationale of infrequent calls and visits. They never really were overly close to me, but what about their brother?

Monday, May 19, 1986

When I came home from work today, Raymond was in bed with a short-sleeve shirt on and a long-sleeve one on over it. His stomach or abdomen looked distended or swollen. He received his ninth radiation treatment to the sacral and back area. His left arm was radiated, and now his right arm is hurting. After I got home, I sent to the store for ice cream. Then I cooked vegetable soup with chicken parts.

Before eating, I took him to get his payroll check. After returning home, he ate a bowl of soup. His right arm hurt so badly, I rubbed it with an over-the-counter analgesic cream. He asked me to put an ace bandage on it, and I did. I encouraged him to take a Darvocet N for pain. He is thin, and walks with his shoulders raised, and his gait is slow. He sleeps in a supine and upright position with three pillows behind his head. Oh, he looks pitiful! As he got on his knees and prayed before retiring, I touched his shoulders and prayed silently for the Lord to heal him or take his soul. Afterwards, I mentioned to him the possibility of Lupron and DES being taken together might be too strong. These medications are given for cancer. He is going downhill fast. I suggested he get another medical opinion. He told me that he'd be going to the doctor Friday for an examination.

He said that he would ask about these cancer medications then. I also mentioned going back to a church healing service. I really don't know what to do. In all of this time, we've never put his name on the church prayer list where we attend. But, I plan to do it this week. Our minister, who works without a ministerial assistant, doesn't usually visit, but he will pray for you.

I called my sister in California to inquire about some colon tests she's having, and to reassure her. She has a mild stomach irritation, and has been on medication. My former boss of ElderCare also called today.

Sunday, May 26, 1986

Raymond's plate is fixed with child-size servings. He eats only about one-third of that, and then has diarrhea after eating. He also has a painful esophagus. He is weak and seemingly afraid of being alone. Kevron, my youngest son, and I went to the store to get another antacid to substitute for the one he is now taking. I also purchased some Kaopectate to help relieve the diarrhea. When we got back, he was in the yard and asked, "Where have you all been?" (New paranoia maybe?) We haven't been to church recently. I hate to go and leave him. He looks chronically ill, being so thin and weak. He received his last radiation treatment of this series Friday. The oncologist did not change his treatment, so the Lupron and DES are continued as before. Every day we watch Raymond go through trials trying to live. He doesn't complain though. I got him to take a prescribed anti-depressant; however, he doesn't like to take them.

Monday, June 2, 1986

I haven't been to work since Thursday. I've been feeling "light headed" and tired. But after getting a return to work slip from the doctor, I returned to work today. Sunday, I went to a swimming party at one of the co-worker's home. Gail, my sister, went with me. We were the only blacks there, and neither of us got into the pool.

Thursday, while I was home with Raymond, I "doctored" his diarrhea that he's been having recently. I gave him his medication and food on time. He got Lomotil, two tablets four times a day, and Imodium after each loose stool. I kept him on a liquid diet, and continued the treatment on Friday. On Saturday, I restarted solid foods, that were bland. He ate creamed potatoes, with no butter or pepper added. He also had boiled chicken seasoned with a little onion and salt. Needless to say, his appetite isn't good. Saturday, we went to a friend's house.

Her daughter is graduating from high school, so I took a card and $10.00. Another neighbor is graduating, so Raymond sent him $10.00 in a card. He has sickle cell anemia. Raymond is spending time in his new recliner he paid nearly $300.00 cash for. How do you tell a real sick person to buy things on time, get insurance, so in the event of severe illness or death, the item would be paid for? I tactfully said to him, "If you buy on time, get insurance on the item, it'll be paid for if your disability check doesn't come through." Well, I can say this for cancer, if it's not one thing, it's another. Raymond vomited Thursday, got nauseated Saturday, but didn't vomit.

On Sunday, I realized both of his lower legs were swollen, so I elevated them on a blanket and pillow. This morning, I gave him a diuretic (Lasix) to decrease the fluid and swelling. Raymond's urinary flow isn't as strong as it should be. I've been giving him Bactrim and Macrodantin by mouth. The drugs were formerly prescribed by an urologist. I give him fluids, especially cranberry juice, to drink. He says that he will be going back to the doctor soon for this urinary problem.

Monday, June 9, 1986

I woke up this morning very angry. Ray, Jr. left for Nashville, Tennessee, last Tuesday. He was to drive from there to Memphis, Tennessee, to attend his girlfriend's brother's wedding. He was to return home Sunday, but he didn't, nor did he call. This has worried Raymond and me all week. This is not like Ray, Jr. at all. We wonder if he arrived safely, or what is going on. He supposedly left a phone number where he could be reached, but I'm unable to find it. Raymond had a brainstorm and told me to look at last month's telephone bill and maybe I could trace Ray, Jr. through the calls he had made. I finally reached Ray, Jr. at his girlfriend's sister's home. All of this is before I cook or get ready for work. Ray, Jr. explained that he hadn't been near a phone, and I learned that he had been involved in a car accident. He mentioned some brake problems in the car he was driving in a heavy rain. His clothes and his ticket to return home were in the wrecked car that was 80 miles away from where he was staying.

There was some question about finances, and Ray, Jr. wanted some money wired to him, but later said that this wouldn't be necessary. Raymond got on the phone and talked sternly: "Ray, I thought you were a better man than that, you haven't called. Now, don't lie, if you're not coming home, don't say you are." Ray, Jr. called back that afternoon very upset over what Raymond had told him earlier. He has always tried so hard to please Raymond.

Raymond went to the doctor today, and received a transfusion of three units of blood again. He was tired and had "gas" upon returning. I gave him an antacid to chew, and a liquid antacid by mouth. I also gave him warm Coke to drink, and he got to feeling better. At supper he ate rice and gravy, liver, and green peas fairly well. He drank Coke. I told him that I would make him a milkshake before bed. He has lost so much weight, and I'm trying to make him gain. He sat in the driveway near the garage of our home and just looked, watching the cars pass, after supper. After returning inside, he went to bed and listened to classical music on the radio.

A friend of the family (very close friend of his sister) sent him a beautiful pair of name brand pajamas. Raymond took the offense, stating that shorts or socks would have done as well. He said, "People expect me to get sick and go to the hospital and need pajamas." He also said, "Being sick is a psychological thing." I assured him by saying, "The pajamas were real nice and expensive, and the gesture was nice." He agreed in part. Now we're awaiting Ray, Jr.'s return home. No doubt all of his air conditioning earnings will be spent on this trip. By the way, we called a toll-free telephone number found in the Lupron literature. We inquired about taking Lupron and DES together, and we were assured that it's OK. That relieved our worries.

Monday, June 16, 1986

Raymond went to the oncologist last Friday (UAB) and the doctors mentioned chemotherapy to him. This depressed him seemingly. So, I told him that this was a suggestion, and that he could pray over it before taking it. I also said, "You have the final decision about what happens to your body." Later, he mentioned visiting the hospital where I work because of its convenient location. I believe he has fear and wants to change doctors again.

Today he heard from Social Security. His disability checks should start in November. His sick pay from U.S. Steel hopefully will continue until this time. Raymond is having some pain in the right shoulder and one hip. He takes a pain pill, Darvocet N, for it. He has Tylenol #3 also, but prefers not to take it because of the codeine in it. Codeine constipates him. He has excessive gas, but by taking antacids before and after meals, this helps. He gets cold quickly. With the temperatures staying in the 80's and 90's, we prefer air conditioning. He keeps a sweater on or around him when it's on.

Yesterday he was thrilled at receiving three Father's Day cards. I bought one for the kids, they bought one, and I gave him one from me with three undershirts and three pairs of shorts. His sister also sent him a card. Today a former school teacher, Mrs. Cook, sent him a card and

$10.00. A neighbor, who peddles vegetables and fruit, sent his truck around and let him pick what he wanted from it.

Another lady in the community gave Ray, Jr. pecans and large white potatoes when he finished working for her. There are good people in this world yet. Uncle Omer's wife, Bea, called to check on us yesterday. Raymond's breathing is shallow seemingly, and he is unshaven. I went to the store and got some razor blades, and encouraged him to shower and shave. I offered to help him, but he refused, stating, "I can do it." There is so much pressure. Ray, Jr.'s car accident will cost him $200.00 (the deductible), plus long distance calls. Ray, Jr. will pay most of it himself. Juan, the second son, wants to go to Kentucky this weekend, supposedly to turn in some lyrics for an upcoming song, and possibly a career change. My! my! my! are my thoughts at this time.

Sunday, June 22, 1986

Raymond went to the doctor Friday. It was thought that he might start chemotherapy, but he didn't. Instead, he was given radiation to the right arm. Raymond called his sister to give her a report. Her minister's wife was visiting, so Raymond left the message with her husband. We rarely hear from his brothers that live here in town. His brothers that live in Milwaukee, Wisconsin, call occasionally.

Yesterday evening, the temperature was 92°. Raymond, Kevron, and I set out to go to the Galleria, a new shopping mall. But, on the way, my brakes became loose, so I stopped at a service station to have them serviced. A young man there tried desperately to help, but couldn't. I probably need brake shoes. I hope no major repairs are needed. Just keeping the air conditioning going in the house, along with other expenses is bothersome. We didn't complete the trip.

Juan's girlfriend came to visit this weekend. Raymond says that the temperature has it too hot upstairs to rest, so he slept downstairs in the recliner. Kevron slept on the couch near him. I was asleep when Kevron came and told me about Raymond sleeping downstairs, but was too tired and sleepy to get up then.

About 5:00 o'clock this morning I got up and went downstairs, only to find Regina and Juan in the living room, sitting on the couch. Neither had gone to bed. Usually Raymond says the house is too cold, but now it's too hot. He seeks comfort any way he can find it. He seems so pitiful--quick to ask things like, "Am I in the way?," or "Please get me a cool drink of water." Now, Raymond and I in some ways have had a somewhat "different" relationship for many years.

I did most of the housework, washing, etc. On holidays, he was usually distant seemingly, and he never took me out on our wedding anniversary. But, he worked hard, paid bills, never fought, and rarely raised his voice. He was often "haughty" somewhat, especially during his mother's lifetime. He is regarded by friends and neighbors as a good husband and father. Now, the children and I are the only ones sticking closely to him. This makes me think deeply.

Monday, June 23, 1986

I slept on the couch downstairs while Raymond slept on the recliner. He got up several times to urinate, and each time I would awaken. I felt so tired when it was time to get up, fix breakfast, and then go to work. When I returned from work, Raymond was sitting on the porch steps--in the sun. He has mentioned how long the day seems when I'm gone. I've repeatedly encouraged him to watch TV, so he told me he watched a re-run detective movie today. We both rested in bed by early nightfall, after eating supper.

He later got up and sat in the living room, where he goes to think deeply, and try to get relief. Gas is a big problem with him still. However, antacids before and after meals help. Someone recommended papaya juice as a remedy for the gas. He drank it and seemingly got better. He was called from University Hospital and was told that his radiation treatments would start Thursday at 10:30 a.m., instead of Tuesday. But now, they will be given in the afternoon instead of mornings.

Saturday, June 28, 1986

Raymond went to the Outpatient Oncology Unit at University Hospital yesterday, and was transfused with two units of blood, making a total of eight that he has received now. The weather is so humid and hot. If the air conditioner stays on any length of time, he becomes chilled and hurt more. He comes up to the bedroom some, maybe lies across the bed, but doesn't sleep in the bed at night. He sleeps in the recliner. He has required more pain killers today.

I went to the beauty shop today. His brother did my hair. My bill was actually $27.00 for a permanent retouch and eyebrow arch. I gave him two $20 bills. He gave me one back.

He also mentioned to me the fact that he gave Raymond $100 once, and Raymond inquired, "What is this for?" He also said that left him with a feeling of not knowing what to do. I don't know if this statement is made out of guilt or sincerity. Raymond's other brother was there, but he never inquires about his brother. They all act peculiar, maybe in an act of denial of his illness. Raymond's radiation treatments to his shoulder have been put off until Monday.

Tuesday, July 1, 1986

This was some kind of day! Yesterday, Raymond had radiation to his right shoulder. Already he has dropped it down some. But, seemingly he's taking more Darvocet N for pain. I worked today. When I returned home, Raymond was sitting up in bed, and told me to sit down and talk to him for a while. So, I did. Yesterday, we went for a walk in the community. This weekend, he mentioned making a will to "protect all of us." I agreed, but later said that it would have to be talked over with a lawyer, since neither of us knows much about wills.

Life is strange--Raymond for years was not very close to me. Often he looked at me with coldness. I told him on several occasions that one day he'd be glad to see me coming, and now, that day has arrived. He told me one day recently, "When you go to work, the time drags, and it's a long time before you come back. I've tried to get him interested in TV programs that will uplift him. Ray, Jr. is taking him for his daily radiation treatments. Oh, it's a blessing for us to have these children. Raymond is asleep in the recliner with a portion of an egg crate mattress under his shoulder. Juanita, a friend of mine, was told recently that she had a malignancy on her back. She is to go to the doctor tomorrow to see about it. Cancer, cancer everywhere, it seems!

Raymond's high school is having a Grand Reunion this week. Many of his friends will be in town. I hope he will attend at least one affair, but so far he isn't enthusiastic. His sister called to inquire about his condition and to invite us to lunch Thursday at her home. The school's banquet will be held later. I'll be working at the time of the luncheon, but maybe Raymond can go.

Friday, July 4, 1986

The country is celebrating the "facelift" of the Statue of Liberty. Last night, Juan barbecued for the family. I cooked baked beans, fixed slaw, and made homemade ice cream today. My sister, Velera's son is visiting Bernard's home for one week. As Bernard and his wife went out, my nephew stayed here with my youngest son, who is enjoying him tremendously. They are nearly the same age.

Juan's girlfriend came for the day. Their lifetime friend, Junior, came over and visited. Raymond and I visited his brother for a while, and went over to Bernard's house (my brother)--as did Kevron. When it was time to come home, Kevron was upset and didn't want to come. I insisted that he come anyway as a teaching mechanism. I told him to have fun, but return home and enjoy your family some, and always throughout your entire life.

Sunday, July 5, 1986

Fairfield Industrial High School's Grand Reunion Picnic is today. Some of his classmates came by and gave him $130.00. There were between 12 and 15 of them. Pictures were taken of the group, and I hope that we can get a copy from one of them. Raymond was uplifted, and verbally told them, "I hate to see you all go." He immediately went to the bathroom after they left, I believe he cried. His sister called and said that she would be to see him on Sunday. I can't believe that he has nephews and brothers here in the city that very rarely visit.

Raymond is certainly going downhill. He has one radiation treatment to get tomorrow, ending this series of five to his shoulder. He is weak, unsteady, and very thin. His appetite is poor. I think that I'll arrange to be off Friday, and go to the doctor with him. If, the boys were not off this summer, what would I do? When they go back to school, all I can see is taking a leave from work, or hiring someone to be here eight hours while I'm away. He certainly can't stay at home alone. I haven't worked this out in my mind yet.

Friday, July 10, 1986

Raymond saw an urologist at Lloyd Noland Hospital today. He said that Raymond's urine looked good. He agreed that Raymond didn't look good, but better than on his last visit.

Saturday, July 11, 1986

Raymond saw an oncologist resident today (at UAB). He appears to be compassionate. He wanted Raymond to continue the therapy of DES by mouth and daily Lupron injections. The DES is to be taken three times daily and the Lupron .2 cc daily. He is also taking Flexeril, a muscle relaxant, three times a day now. The doctor also said that chemotherapy will have to be started if some relief is not obtained from the present medications. Raymond is miserable for sure!

He holds his shoulders the way a person with congenital deformities would. He weighed 152.5 pounds today, but when he became ill, he weighed 210 pounds. I bought Ensure, a dietary supplement, and he drank one. Later, he complained of gas pains. I then gave him room temperature Coke to drink, and sodium bicarbonate later. Also, Gaviscon has been given for gas. He now wants a hospital bed. He feels that it would be more comfortable than our bed.

Monday, July 12, 1986

I went to pay the last house mortgage payment today. No one was there who could answer questions about insurance coverage on the house after the mortgage is paid in full. So, this trip downtown was practically for nothing. I had the drapes in the den cleaned, so they were picked up today. Also, I put four shirts in the laundry for Raymond: going to the doctor so often necessitates many clean clothes. I also took Raymond to the doctor, went to the credit union, and made a deposit in the savings account. Raymond went back to the car only to have it not start at first. Later, it did. Also later, I bought grocery. To add to all the frustrations, I broke a front tooth--my, this was a full day.

Chapter Six

HOSPITALIZATION FOR NECK PROBLEMS (JULY) AND POST-SURGERY

Tuesday, July 13, 1986

Raymond is in considerable pain, especially around his shoulders. As he stood up once, he leaned backward and he had to pull his neck up off of his chin and chest. This prompted a trip to the Emergency Room at the University of Alabama at Birmingham. The doctors and nurses were nice enough, and explained the visitation rules of the Emergency Room. I had to stay in the waiting room until they paged me to come in to talk with the doctors after the examination was completed.

After the examination, Raymond had a prescription for Tylenol #3, a note to apply a heating pad to his back, return to the Emergency Room if his condition worsened. But, I refused to take Raymond home without questioning if his neck or back was broken. This question seemingly startled the doctor. He told me that he didn't take any X-rays, but that he would "if you insist." After the X-rays were done (at my request), I noticed that something was wrong. They came in with a Philadelphia neck collar, and repeated instructions to "lie still."

They sent for X-rays that were taken in May, so comparisons could be made. They found much spread of cancer to the neck. The neck bones were twisted and they marveled at the fact that the spinal cord wasn't severed, or his respirations weren't depressed enough for instant respiratory failure and death. He was admitted to the oncology floor, Room W-912, in traction to his head with two pounds of weights attached for immobilization. I called a co-worker to contact my boss and report me off from work. For now, Raymond must be fed, bathed, and handed the urinal to pass water, etc.

Monday, July 14, 1986

Raymond is not in pain, but remains in traction. There is talk of surgery for his neck- -five fractured bones. I was alarmed. Is he able to tolerate surgery? Is surgery necessary?

Can another form of treatment be given? I didn't want to hurt anyone's feelings. There is a very competent neurosurgeon on Raymond's case (Dr. Lankford) and an orthopedist (Dr. Dunham) that will work with him. I sent for another neurosurgeon (Dr. Morowitz) for a second opinion. He works some at the hospital where I work, and has done much surgery on a co-worker. He comes highly recommended, and I value his advice. He basically agreed that surgery is the treatment of choice. But, cobalt treatments might be given if surgery is declined. I still have reservations.

Tuesday, July 15, 1986

I called my boss for additional time off from work. It's a hectic time in ElderCare. The other nurse in my department will be on vacation, and my boss will be leaving after Thursday, and is to be married July 19th. One of my co-workers sent Raymond a beautiful plant. He had many evening visitors, including his sister and her husband; his brother, Al; and our children. Later Raymond became restless and painful. I think it was due some to overstimulation and too many visitors. My son, Juan, who left last week to go back to Nashville, Tennessee, had car trouble 60 miles before reaching his destination, and had to be towed in to Nashville. So, today after I wired him some money, he came home.

After I left the hospital, I called Raymond's brother, Al, to see if he thought his brother should have surgery. He spoke of the divine being and prayer. He advised me to talk thoroughly with the doctor. But after I prayed, a song came to me--"I Surrender All," and it stayed with me and my thoughts.

Wednesday, July 16, 1986

Surgery is planned for tomorrow. Bone is to be taken from the iliac crest and be transplanted to the neck with wires to hold the neck together. I was shocked today at what Raymond told me. He said that he worries about his soul sometimes. He called the church, talked to a receptionist, telling her of his impending surgery, and requested the pastor's prayers. The pastor is preaching a revival in Gadsden, but stopped by the hospital on his way there. He prayed a good prayer, and rubbed the right side of Raymond's neck with his hand. Mrs. Nevett, his wife, also called and talked. I've always liked the Nevetts.

Raymond ate and ate after he found out that he cannot have food and water after midnight. He received a sleeping pill, and by 12:08 a.m. he was very sleepy. He has a lot of fear, and our pastor suggested that he read a scripture from 1st Corinthians, and after he read it, he asked me if the pastor thought that he was going to die.

At home, my sister, Gail, went over and put the drapes up in the basement, cooked, and cleaned after cleaning her house. She is not too physically strong or healthy, so I hated for her to do all of this. She did a wonderful job. I dread tomorrow, but have hopes that everything will be alright.

Friday, July 18, 1986

Raymond had surgery on his cervical spine yesterday. Nine hours of suspense and trauma! When he did come out of surgery and the recovery room, he was alert, but had some swelling or edema of the face. A drainage bag (hemovac) was connected to the right side of his neck, and two bottles of intravenous fluids were going. The doctors kept me posted or updated as I sat in the Surgical Waiting Room during the surgery.

The first call came approximately after five hours of surgery, the time the doctors predicted that it would end. I received another call one and one-half hours later. It seems that the procedure, fusion of the cervical spine with the bone graft, is very tedious due to the cancerous state of the bone they have to work with. The attempt to secure bone from the iliac crest failed due to this, then the fibula bone (leg) was used. He was transfused blood in surgery, but I don't know how many units were used.

The unit or room where he was preoperatively (before surgery) called the waiting room and said that Raymond's belongings should be moved because he would be going to NICU (Neuro-Intensive Care Unit). The Surgical Waiting Room closed at 4:30 p.m., so I went up to the Neuro-Intensive Care area to wait for him. There I learned that he wouldn't be coming there after all, but would go to 6 South, a dingy-looking floor in a semi-private room yet. I was appalled. I objected vigorously. So, they put him in a large room across from the nurses' station. He wasn't there an hour before an elderly white gentleman coded (hospital jargon for extreme emergencies) and died. I didn't think Raymond was alert enough to know that he died. We had the curtains pulled. Many times, the nurses tried to get me to leave the room while they worked on the old gentleman, but I didn't because the staff was all tied up with him during the code. Raymond had thick mucous in his throat that required suctioning and constant spitting. Oxygen was going via an open face mask at 40%. If I didn't stay with my husband, I felt that he might have chocked or needed attention with no one to give it to him. I again asked for a private room, and was finally moved to the 15th floor (Neurosurgery wing), only to be put in a semi-private room. However, the other bed was empty. So, I went on in, with the request to be moved when a private room became available on the same floor. My concern was that sometimes in a semi-private room, the other person is real sick and requires much attention, not allowing anyone adequate rest. Secondly, the wife, if the other patient is married often objects to another woman being in the room with her sick husband due to possible exposure. The mix-up with the semi-private and private rooms occurs in all hospitals, but seemingly more readily in a large hospital like Raymond is in now. But, finally, after I got home to rest some, Raymond was moved to a private room.

My brothers, Leon and Bernard, came to visit. My brother who works at the complex where my husband is hospitalized wanted to call the Administrator concerning the room problems, but I objected. I've worked in hospitals long enough to know that you don't make waves if at all possible. Somehow, I wonder if he went to the Administrator anyway. The neurosurgery staff is very attentive, and even cleaned the private room before we moved, waxed the floor and everything. Anyway, Raymond was put up in a chair today, ate well and looked good, but made the comment, "Look like cancer is catching up with me."

Physical therapy was started, and the nurses taught him to use the incentive spirometer, a devise to aid in keeping the lungs expanded and free of pneumonia and other medical problems. When I left the hospital, I had intentions of going back after working some around the house (washing, cooking, etc.). I didn't rest enough to go back, so Ray, Jr. went and stayed. I understand from Ray, Jr., his daddy is having pains that he refers to as "spasms," but I'm sure they're only post-operative pains combined with the cancer. He was told today the he would need radiation to his neck starting Monday. The Lupron and DES have been stopped. I've asked the nurses to get that straight, but I'll get back on it tomorrow. Apparently, chemotherapy will have to start! I hope it isn't too late. How can they stop the anti-cancer drugs now? I'm upset and confused. This is a tiring, trying time for me. I stopped by to see my friend who has a form of skin cancer, but she was in surgery. I'll stop by to see her in the morning--cancer, cancer everywhere, I thought.

Friday, July 25, 1986

I'm in Raymond's hospital room, and have been since 10:00 a.m. yesterday. Food, along with parking, etc., is expensive. Parking in the hospital deck with no meter to contend with is $3.00 a day. The average meal is $2.50. Raymond's intravenous fluids are going at K.V.O. (keep vein open) rate. His antibiotic has been changed from Ancef to Vancamycin. His temperature went up to over 101° at midnight, but after getting a sleeping pill and two Tylenol tablets, he slept fairly well.

Yesterday, a co-worker of my sister, Gail, came by and prayed. She is a minister and healer, as well as a teacher. There were many tears, anointing and praises for God. I am to return to work Monday. I'm trying to figure out a family schedule that's workable, and will allow everyone adequate rest, and afford Raymond constant companionship.

Thursday, July 31, 1986 (10:15 p.m.)

The doctors have come and gone for the day. They removed sutures from his hip, legs, and neck. His temperature at 8:00 p.m. was 99.8° orally. They are planning to send him home soon. They even asked if he wanted to leave tomorrow. Last Saturday, his temperature went up to 104°. He didn't show any more symptoms. Blood and urine cultures were done, as was a chest X-ray. Later I found out that the blood cultures were negative. I'll have to find out later about the urine culture and the chest X-ray. Doctors don't readily volunteer this information if not asked, seemingly.

Yesterday, Mary Sanders, a family friend, cooked a large dinner for my boys. The boys stopped at her home and ate blackeyed peas, cabbage, dressing and chicken, candied yams, and cake. That was a nice gesture. Friends are such help in times like these.

Saturday, August 2, 1986

Al, Raymond's brother, spent a night with Raymond. Raymond was restless, he said, and his temperature went to 102°. Raymond was nervous. Blood and wound cultures were done. I relieved Al at 8:15 a.m. He left $15 for TV service, and I was so appreciative that he stayed. I slept well, and got up and fixed breakfast before returning to the hospital. I bathed Raymond after he ate, and he then went to physical therapy and was worked out for one hour approximately. He returned to physical therapy again at 2:00 p.m. Several doctors, nurses, and doctor assistants have visited, checking on drainage from Raymond's wound, sending a wound culture to the lab. Tylenol has been given for his elevated temperature, and Tylox has been given for pain, after his second trip to physical therapy. It seems to them, the temperature elevation is due to a wound infection of the neck.

Sunday, August 3, 1986

Raymond came home Friday night late. He was transfused with blood, got his antibiotics, and was released with a Hickman catheter intact. The purpose of the catheter is to give medications and draw blood without much fanfare or pain to the patient. As a nurse, I never liked working with Hickman catheters. It's scary knowing how vulnerable one is to infections when one is present, and also the possibility of hemorrhage.

His temperature remains up to 104° at most times. Once at 4:00 a.m., it dropped to 98°. His appetite is good. His gait is bent and unsteady. He is very weak. The Philadelphia collar (neck collar) is intact. His sister, Alvis, came by today and snapped some beans for me to cook. Yesterday, she sent two new sheets for Raymond's bed. Also, today a co-worker from U.S. Steel came by to see him, as he lay in the hospital bed. The president of the company that leased me the bed grew up in the same community as I did. He threw in a free bedside commode, and billed me $82 for a month. I will send him the check in the morning. Help comes from unexpected sources.

Chapter Seven

HOSPITALIZATION: AUGUST 5 - 15, 1986 AND POST-CARE

Friday, August 8, 1986

Raymond was admitted to the hospital again on August 5, 1986, after being discharged August 1st. This admission was due to a distended (swollen) abdomen or stomach, and the loss of the use of his legs. He was taken to the Emergency Room at the advice of a female neurosurgeon on call there (Dr. Thomas), and also on the advice of a doctor at Lloyd Noland Hospital after I discussed the symptoms with him.

The admitting doctor thought that the distended abdomen might be due to an ileus or an obstruction of the intestines. After spinal X-rays were done, it was decided that the tumors have spread and are pressing against the spinal column. He was admitted to Room 1506, a private room, kept NPO (nothing by mouth), intravenous fluids were started, and his bed kept flat. He is visibly shaken over not being able to move his legs. He states, "This means a wheelchair."

A catheter was inserted into his bladder, and afterwards, his abdomen began to go down. On Wednesday morning (1:00 a.m.), tests were done that included a myelogram and repeat Cat scans, and also, a radiation treatment. His sister left for a trip Wednesday, but visited him before leaving. She was so upset and said, "I hate to leave Raymond laying here like that." She had tears in her eyes. After she left the room, Raymond cried and said, "Things aren't going right." He asked me to sing with him, "I Surrender All" and "Just As I Am." I sang as I was asked, and then prayed aloud with him. He seems to get much solace when I sing and pray with him.

On Wednesday and Thursday nights, a neighbor of my deceased mother stayed with him for 10 hours each night for $3.60 an hour. This morning, a little movement is noted in his legs again. A friend of his sister (Mrs. Yarborough) stayed with him while I worked today. She is a retired Registered Nurse, and I feel good when she's around.

Saturday, August 9, 1986

I've been here at the hospital for over 24 hours. Raymond ate fairly well today, but his voice is weakening. His legs seem to have function returning to them slowly. After eating prunes for breakfast, and the nurses giving him medication that included a Dulcolax suppository, diarrhea has become a problem. He had five stools, and his buttocks are becoming sore. They have ordered Sween Cream for his buttocks. I also asked them to give him something to decrease the bowel movements. He complained of severe back pains, and two Percodan tablets were given him. He rested some after taking this medication. His temperature ranges from between 97° and 98° today, and he is in fairly good spirits. Each time he has a stool, he asks me to give him leg exercises. He knows I'll find the stool if I lift his legs, and this is a tactful way for him to ask for help in getting clean.

We watched several TV programs, and he remarked, "We haven't prayed aloud today." I planned to, but he would fall asleep each time before I had a chance. Finally, we did.

It rained some, and he wanted to look out at it, but it was difficult for me to get the bed turned so that he could see. He made the remark, "You're tired now, and can't think well." He appears to be so worried that I'll get too tired. He becomes almost hysterical if he has an accident in bed, and I try change the linen alone. He wants me to call the floor nurses, and perhaps I should. Being a nurse myself, I know the shortage of staff nurses, so, I'll proceed to help out. Tomorrow I plan to stay at home and rest some. I have so much hope for Raymond. Some of the nurses seem concerned about me working and staying at the hospital so much. They are fearful of my rest and eating habits.

Tuesday, August 19, 1986

A lot of water has gone under or over the dam since I last wrote a diary note. Raymond was discharged from the hospital (UAB) August 15, 1986. A former outpatient clinic appointment made before his hospital admission was cancelled. He received most of his radiation treatments while hospitalized, but had to return for radiation treatments Monday, August 18th, and Tuesday, August 19th. He is to return to the hospital on August 22nd for an abdominal sonogram (X-ray), and he has an appointment to return to the hospital on September 10, 1986, to see the neurosurgeon (Dr. Lankford). Recently, he had problems with sore throats. He is able to move his legs, but is unable to stand or walk, which worries him greatly.

He expressed a desire to see the oncologist at Lloyd Noland Hospital where I work. It is much closer to home. A nurse, Effie, started working with him yesterday. She works with the Augmentation Nursing Agency. She and I worked together formerly at Lloyd Noland Hospital. We always had a good rapport. She is a licensed practical nurse, and lives in the same vicinity as us. Raymond seems to have confidence in her. Her supervisor calls and seems to take an active interest in Raymond's welfare. Raymond's bowels are a problem. He was given enemas by me Sunday and Tuesday. Effie put him on the bedside commode Monday, and he had a large bowel movement. His appetite is good, and he is glad to be out of the hospital. I sleep in a bed next to his, but he has fears. He is fearful of falling or of someone not hearing him when he calls or needs help.

Wednesday, August 20, 1986

I told Raymond this morning to stop worrying or being fearful. I explained to him that I only would do what's best for him at all times. I did this before leaving for work, and after cooking his breakfast. When I returned from work, he was in a good mood. But, he was experiencing gas. I put him on the bedpan and gave him a fleets enema that he was unable to hold. So, later I gave him a suppository in his rectum that did no good. So, later, I gave him a soap suds enema, and large amounts of stool returned. He was relieved and ate, ate, ate after that.

He craves and eats sweets such as candy bars. He has it at his bedside, but I'm afraid that he'll develop diabetes on top of everything else. A Hoyer lift was delivered yesterday, and is a big help in lifting him and moving him about. After getting up via the lift, his fear of falling seems less. Before coming home, I stopped by his workplace office and picked up his check. With the strike or walkout being in process, and with new personnel filling in, no check was originated from Pittsburgh for him. An estimated check of $540.00 was issued. Ray, Jr. deposited the check.

Juan is leaving for school today, and appears anxious to do so. I went to bed at 10:00 a.m. this morning, and Juan had not come in yet. So, he'll be traveling to school without much rest. There's so much to make me anxious--home, work, and the boys.

Tuesday, September 2, 1986

What a bang to start the work week out with! Raymond's urine bag was emptied, his Hickman catheter was flushed with Heparin to keep it from clogging up, equipment was given to him to shave. Breakfast was served which consisted of an over light egg and hard toast at his request, coffee, and oatmeal. He ate well. Effie came to start her day's work, and when I got into my car, it wouldn't start. Effie immediately gave me her car keys and off I went. I got to work at 8:05 a.m. Later I found out that it was the battery that had gone bad in my car.

Yesterday was Labor Day, and I was home. So, today was the beginning of the week for me, in a sense. Ray, Jr. left for school at about 5:30 p.m., so he could catch the bus at 6:00 p.m. He called later stating that he had gotten there. He was such a big help to me, but in a way I'm relieved. He is young, and is under pressure. He would date until 3:00 a.m., using my car, and usually keeping the gas tank nearly empty. Juan left for school over a week ago. I'm glad that they are good boys.

Raymond's leg activity is better, but he constantly complains of a sore throat. I wonder if it is the cancerous process, or is it post-radiation therapy? His overall condition is pretty good right now. He has a small sore area on his sacrum (back) that I've used Betadine solution and ointment on. Also, I've tried Methiolate and Maalox without improvement. Now, I'm trying Bard protective barrier on it.

This afternoon the physical therapist came by for the second visit today. He didn't stay long, but did well while here. He's coming to our home.

Wednesday, September 3, 1986

I'm in a precarious position, Raymond is alert enough to run business as usual, but not well enough to do so. He still wants to be in on all decision making. He has poor judgment at times. He takes medication, and doesn't think as clearly as a well person. He worries a lot, becomes easily confused and overwhelmed. He worried all night about getting up in the Hoyer lift today, since this is his laxative-taking day (Sorbital 30 ccs). Some other skin abrasions were found on him yesterday, so I cut the eggcrate cushion he sits on, putting a hole in the cushion to match the hole in the canvas of the Hoyer lift. This gives him a smooth, soft edge to sit on. At 10:00 a.m., when I called home, he was up, but our prior agreement was for him to stay in bed until time for a bowel movement which is usually three hours after he takes the Sorbital. He is getting where he doesn't remember well, and he puts pressure on Effie to comply with his wishes.

His throat remains sore. I'm going to check with the oncologist at Lloyd Noland Hospital to secure another prescription for Percodan if possible. I checked with medical records where I work, and they have not received records from Raymond's previous hospitalization at UAB. I called the social worker at UAB to see if forms could be mailed so I can take them to U.S. Steel, thus restarting money that we need (from Raymond's place of employment).

Tuesday, September 9, 1986

For the last two weeks, things have gone along as usual--caring for Raymond before and after work, with Effie working eight hours while I work. She writes nursing notes and leaves them so that I can read them. Sunday, a neighbor, Mrs. McKinney, visited and left a donation of $20.00. Aunt Bea and Uncle Sut came by and left a donation of $15.00.

Today was the day Raymond received Sorbital, a laxative. He dreads taking it in a way, wondering if he'll mess up the sheets or have a fecal impaction present, as he usually does. Some church members came by while I was at work and left $4.00.

I went by U.S. Steel's Union Hall yesterday to inquire about insurance the Union is preparing since the strike or walkout is in process. Last Thursday I received a disturbing letter stating that medical and dental insurance is now cancelled. I have nurses, medical equipment, and a very sick husband, with no insurance. How can this be?, I ask.

My brother, Bernard, went to UAB to pick up forms signed by the neurosurgeon, to aid Raymond in getting disability and to reinstate benefits now cut off. The office is trying hard to get him qualified for disability by the end of the month. As I write this, Raymond is asleep, his mouth open and also his eyes. His skin is clammy (moist and cool). I am so depressed!

Raymond is so pitiful the way he asks can I have this or can I have that, like a little child. This once strong-willed man is now like a newborn baby. He gets up when we get him up, and eats when we bring him food, and we exercise his extremities as we choose to do it. He is to see the neurosurgeon tomorrow, and he will see Dr. Pineda, the oncologist, on Friday for blood transfusion (at Lloyd Noland Hospital).

Saturday, September 13, 1986

This is beginning to be somewhat of a funny weekend. I hurried about washing, cooking, and cleaning. Grocery shopping was done last night. Today is Raymond's day to get a laxative, since he gets it every other day. He expelled feces easily with the help of an enema. I left him in bed to drain (on the bedpan) while I went to the store to purchase underpads for the bed. I needed a new commode seat for the master bathroom, and a "for sale" sign for Ray, Jr.'s car. After purchasing this and hurrying home, I found my aunt and her children from Mississippi visiting. They had folded my clothes that I washed when I returned. That one thing was such a tremendous help to me.

Sunday, September 14, 1986

As we were putting Raymond in bed with the Hoyer lift--referred to by him as the hoist--his catheter from the bladder came out inflated. Apparently, we had pulled on it in some way. I found the phone book, checked the yellow pages, and found a pharmacy open on Sunday. It was located in West End. I traveled there and got a catheter. As I put it in and inflated it, a blister rose up on the outside of the catheter, rendering it unusable after the blister ruptured. I've inserted many foley catheters and never saw one do that.

I then called a pharmacy in Ensley, closer to where I live, and found that they had catheters. I went there and got one and inserted it. As I traveled there, I've never felt so helpless, so bewildered in all my life. I prayed all the way for strength to go on. I felt like I was being tried like Job in the Bible. After all was over, Raymond ate a fair amount of lunch. The menu included fresh turnip greens, squash, cornbread, roast beef, and chocolate cake. He is expecting his sister to visit tomorrow for the first time in a month. She has been ill with bronchitis, she says, and will wear a mask during the visit to keep Raymond from becoming infected. One of Raymond's brothers is in the hospital in Milwaukee, Wisconsin. He has urinary problems. This fact seemingly depressed Raymond. He is encouraging his sisters and brothers to have him have prostate surgery if needed, and not risk "suffering like I have." At 12:42 a.m. the next morning, Raymond is eating oatmeal cookies and drinking root beer soda.

Chapter Eight

HOSPITALIZATION: SEPTEMBER 18, 1986 AND POST-CARE

Friday, September 19, 1986

You know, I have so much to write now until I don't know where to start. For starters, Raymond was admitted to the hospital on September 18, 1986. I called a doctor on call for the oncologist to get permission to bring Raymond to the hospital. This is part of the protocol, noted in the insurance that we have joined through our Health Maintenance Organization (HMO) Plan. Consequently, he was admitted. The ambulance attendant took his temperature, and got a reading of 104°.

Diagnosis-U.T.I. (urinary tract infection). He was admitted to Room 224-B, at Lloyd Noland Hospital. The floor on which he was admitted was nice, with a competent, hardworking staff. Kevron, my youngest child, was a constant companion. We left the hospital at 3:00 a.m. the following morning. He didn't go to school, nor I to work the following day. We rested some, and got up to the hospital about 11:00 a.m. When we arrived, Raymond was clean and wild looking. His hair had not been combed. I combed it, and after being there for a while, he began to calm down. His sister came by after work today, and one of his brothers came to the Emergency Room last night to be with us.

One big problem facing me now is the strike or "lock out" at U.S. Steel. You see, Raymond was ill prior to this, and his name has been left off of the benefits form. I've been told that the union is to help with this problem. I took off today and went to the Flintridge Building, and waited on Mr. Rich, who listened attentively to the problem and promised to help. One of Raymond's co-workers came to the hospital with a copy of the union contract, and emergency-type plan set up by the union during this time. He offered to help in any way he could.

One night last week, I think Monday, Raymond said to me, "I love you," after I cut the light off and went to bed. I love him too, very much.

All of my siblings that live close by called me today. One of my brothers, Bernard, informed me that Juan, my second oldest son, is coming home tomorrow. Now, I feel obligated to call and let them know that their daddy is in the hospital, so Ray, Jr. can come also if he wants.

Tuesday, September 23, 1986

Raymond is mentally confused, talking irrationally at times, and feeling that he is deserted. I've hired a sitter to stay with him from 11:00 p.m. to 7:00 a.m., while I rest. It costs $4.00 an hour. With all of the bills mounting, I don't know the outcome of this, but I'm living on faith. Gifts come in, and how they help! Five dollars from the male chorus, one dollar from a friend, etc.

Raymond asked the sitter to pull the curtains back so that he could see when I go to work. He says that he has, "something to work out with her." He is saying this because I did not stay with him last night. The same evening, I went home to check on the house, buy some needed items, and he refused supper. From now on, I've decided, I'll stick around at meal times. This encourages him to eat, it seems. The oncologist says that he will keep Raymond through this week, possibly to the weekend. I feel the worst. Bed sores that have started are now being healed. They are being treated with Granulex, a substance that's sprayed on them.

After completing my chores at home, I returned to the hospital with fried chicken wings and french fries that I purchased from Jack's. He ate a wing and some french fries, and drank apple juice. He becomes confused and upset each time I leave the hospital. But as hard as I try, I can't stay all of the time. Even when I'm working, I try to be present at mealtimes, and as much as possible.

Friday, September 26, 1986 (7:15 p.m.)

I'm still here at the hospital, after coming early this morning and working too. I brought a piece of his brace that I left in the car yesterday. He told me, "I'm confused and afraid to close my eyes." After I arrive and stay a while, a calm peace seems to appear.

Today, my co-worker and I were working "on the field" at a senior citizens site, screening for blood pressure and blood sugar problems. My co-worker gave a short lecture. When I got back to the hospital, I stopped by to see Raymond before returning to my workplace. Immediately, he blurted out, "Vertis, how can you do this to me? You left me scared. I'm scared to close my eyes, I might die. I don't want to go down to the devil." I said, "You're a

Christian, aren't you?" He said, "Yes, but it's not that simple when you're all bound down like me. I have this catheter on, and I'm bound down. Look at my feet--I can't walk."

Today, I received a card from my mission sisters at church with $50 in it. Kevron's Boy Scout Troop sent a card with $15 in it. I praised God for the Carnation Circle and Troop #154.

Raymond is so fearful. I asked my sister, Gail, to go to my home and get Kevron. She is to either bring him to the hospital or take him to her home. This allowed me to stay at Raymond's bedside. He slept soundly part of the time.

Saturday, September 27, 1986

His temperature at 11:00 a.m. today is 102°. Tylenol was given for the fever. He complained of neck pain, and Tylox was given. He sleeps off and on, and his voice is a whisper. He seems to be slipping fast! However, the oncologist believes that he will be discharged on Monday or Tuesday after receiving another blood transfusion. Somehow, I just don't believe it! I left the hospital to buy grocery, and to get clothes to wear tomorrow. Bernard has Kevron, and will take him to church tomorrow. I appreciate this kind of help so much. Somehow, the fear is leaving Raymond now. I'm leading him in prayer--"Lord, save my soul, forgive me for my sins." He complains bitterly at times with neck pain. His temperature at 10:00 p.m. is 98.6°. He is lethargic. I'm scared the end is near! He told me not to tell the boys, "what shape I'm in." "Let them stay up there in school," he said.

Thursday, October 2, 1986

I talked with Dr. Pineda (the oncologist) this morning. Raymond is to go home tomorrow if everything is alright. He is mentally confused, and the thought of going home has worsened it seemingly. His sister came by after work, and was gone when I got off from work at 4:30 p.m. His older brother visited Thursday night, after nearly two weeks of Raymond's hospitalization. The oncologist revealed to me that a meningioma (or benign brain tumor) was found after they did tests. He said that it probably was present since childhood. Tuesday night, Raymond had a temperature of 103°, and was very sick.

The house doctor (or doctor on call) was called in. He ordered blood cultures, a chest X-ray, and Tylenol was given for the elevated temperature and hard chill. Raymond admitted to being nervous and scared. He once whispered to me, "Am I in the basement?" He also asked questions with frowns on his face and distress in his voice. He prays for the Lord to come and get him. He is so distressed! The question, "How am I going to get home?" is asked frequently. "I didn't think I'd ever get home," he says. "Can you get me up when I get home?" Can I have my leg fixed so we can be normal?" "Why do you have me like this?" (positioned on his left side). These questions and comments go on and on.

Friday, October 3, 1986

Raymond was discharged as usual today. Effie, the nurse, followed the ambulance home, and took care of Raymond until I got off from work and came home.

Saturday, October 4, 1986

I had business as usual today. I got my hair shampooed at 4:30 p.m. Afterwards, I delivered a check to Raymond's nephew's home, clearing up an air conditioning job that resulted in problems. Raymond had been involved in this problem for one year. Later, I picked up groceries. When I did return, both Raymond and Kevron were frantic. Uncle Sut (paternal uncle) and Uncle Booker (maternal uncle) visited together, leaving some money behind to help out. Later, a neighbor came by with fruit for Raymond. His father sells fruit on a truck.

Sunday, October 5, 1986

I got up early, and bathed Raymond well. Visitors and calls came in. Raymond ate poorly at lunch time. Included in the visitors today were Raymond's sister and brother, and his brother's wife. A neighbor that brought $25, and Kevron's Scout Master, Mr. Montgomery.

At night Raymond becomes confused. He called out loudly, "Lady, lady," to get attention. Today, he said that his daddy would be coming to get him.

Monday, October 6, 1986

I went to the store with a neighbor for a short while today. I believe that she is trying to give me a "breather" when she asked me to go with her. When I returned after a short stay,

Raymond couldn't talk--only mumble. He acted like a stroke victim. I think he was upset! But, he ate one-half bowl of potato soup, two pieces of fish fillets, one-half glass of Coke, and one-half cup of chocolate pudding. Afterwards, he calmed down. Off an on, he calls out with pain, especially if the catheter isn't draining well.

Now, he has a condom catheter on, instead of a Foley catheter--less chance for urinary tract infections. He says, "Vertis" with such fervor, usually three times for emphasis. Tylenol is given every four hours around the clock, he stools at night, and frequently asks for water. He asks to be turned over frequently also. His room at home is set up like a hospital room. He has an overbed table that raises up and down, medications to take, and those for skin care close by. Fresh water is near. I often wonder how long I can work at the hospital and hold up to these responsibilities at home.

Monday, October 13, 1986

We had many visitors yesterday, including our minister's wife, Mrs. Nevett. Raymond's brother, Al, called and mentioned a rumor he had heard that Raymond was dead. A doctor at Lloyd Noland Hospital had heard the same rumor. This left me edgy all day. The pain medication, Percodan, that is being given to Raymond every four hours is given in conjunction with Tylenol. When I visited the doctors today, I asked for a sleeping pill for him, and samples of Dalmane 30mg were given to me. I was up five times during the night, so I hope the sleeping pills will lessen this. Among the visitors on yesterday, was my sister, who commented how tired I looked.

Raymond's color is ashen, his respirations are shallow at times. When I administered the Dalmane capsule, I poured some of it out by opening the capsule and putting it back together. I'm afraid the sleeping pill, along with his pain medication and Tylenol, will be too much.

Ray, Jr. left for school at 8:00 p.m., with instructions to call back when he arrived. The choir members collected $43 dollars and sent it down today by a member.

I think now, "How good it is to belong to church organizations." When I mentioned the death rumor to Raymond's nurse, who stays with him while I work, she made me think of its possible origin: On October 3rd, we took Raymond to the doctor, and it was raining some. So we covered his head until getting him into the ambulance. Some neighbors saw us, as did passer-bys in cars. I guess she was right!

Tuesday, October 21, 1986

So much has happened since I had a chance to write. Saturday night, we sang songs at his request: "I Surrender All" and "Amazing Grace." During the day, two church members (one, a graduate of the same nursing school as me) stayed with Raymond while I got my hair washed and shopped for groceries. Now, he's on Morphine Elixir by mouth for pain, is more rational, and less painful at the moment.

Sunday, Mr. McCoy, the Jehovah Witness, came by, and read and talked with Raymond. Last night, Mrs. Dunner, a teacher and co-worker of my sister, came by with her husband (both are ministers). They gave us some "blessed" soap to bathe Raymond in. A United Steel spokeslady called and assured us that they are trying to get Raymond on disability soon.

I still have to get up four to five times at night to "pull my feet out, turn me over, I want some water," etc. His sister called tonight saying that she will come by tomorrow and bring some pecans that Raymond likes to eat. She mentioned that she cannot stay long when she comes because her husband is out of town. I feel very tired, and started to stay home today, but I didn't. I keep pushing on and on, praying all of the way.

Raymond's nurse made an entry in the nurse's notes stating, "Raymond is depressed." He wouldn't eat much for her, but when I came home and cooked, he ate a whole pork chop, rice and gravy, fresh spinach, and one-half bowl of soup. As a matter of fact, he could hardly wait for me to cook. He accused me of eating my dinner before bringing his upstairs to him. Of course, this isn't true.

Kevron, the youngest son, is argumentative and pouty. He wants a gun that I refuse to buy. Bernard is to pick him up Saturday for a "breather," and he needs it. Watching his daddy suffer is certainly affecting him. My younger brother's, Leon, home was broken into as he worked. Many of his precious items were stolen. My, my, problems everywhere!

Friday, October 24, 1986 (4:00 a.m.)

"Let me in, let me in," I heard when I awoke and came to my senses. Raymond was very, very upset, thinking that I was his sister when I got up and went over to his bed. He continued to talk, "I thought we were the close ones, You know daddy wouldn't like it about you doing me like this." Somehow, he felt that he was outside knocking, trying to get inside. Apparently, this is a regression back to teenage or young adulthood years. Last week he made a comment about how he loves his mama and daddy.

Monday, when I cooked pork chops, he asked me if I had steamed them. Then he went on to say, "Boy, mama could cook these things." Everything now seems to be centered around his childhood.

It's hard to see after a sick person and work. Sometimes I think of hiring a nurse at night, but think of how expensive it is. I plan to stay off work today, but being one of only two nurses in the department, I went on. The other nurse has injured her foot. Also, one of the medical secretaries is off sick, and our department has a small staff anyway.

Raymond's temperature is down to normal this morning. I take it each day before leaving for work. Yesterday, it went up to 102.2°. I asked the urologist for an antibiotic, and he quickly responded by calling in a prescription for Duracef, to be taken by mouth. The oncologist wrote another prescription for Morphine also, so it can be continued.

Tuesday, October 28, 1986

Raymond babbles and babbles constantly, sleeping very little. He calls me "mama," and by the name of his two sisters--one of whom is deceased. He becomes verbally abusive at times, and cries at times. He mentions seeing numbers coming out of the sky. He wants me to request the present minister of the church I grew up in (Metropolitan C.M.E) to pray for him. He also wants the minister of the church we presently attend to pray for him. He says things like, "You know, I can't continue like this. I'm going to eventually die." Today, at work, I asked the oncologist for medicine to calm him, and he prescribed Haldol. After taking it, I could see a change--it helped. However, he asked for his legs to be turned aloose, and he asked for water often. Some of the medication he takes seems to make his mouth very dry.

I am having trouble with pain, and seemingly a knot in my left breast. My pap smear is delinquent, but I don't--or won't--take time to see about these things now.

Ray, Jr. and Juan visited this weekend, and certainly were a big help to me. They help so much in the care of their daddy when they are here. I worry about the pressure they're under trying to study and worry about their father simultaneously.

The hospice nurse comes by twice weekly, and gives suggestions for his care. The hospice nurse was the one who initiated the prescription for Morphine, and even gave me some to give him. The pain appears much less now that he's taking it.

Wednesday, October 29, 1986

Raymond's Foley catheter was changed to a silicone one, size 18. The hospice nurse states that they work better. When it was inserted, 400 cc of thick urine came out immediately. However, the previous catheter seemed to have been working. Thoughts come and go in my mind. Is he septic, causing this elevated temperature and mental confusion? Has the disease process progressed to his brain? His sister came yesterday, and says that she will return tomorrow. She usually comes when I'm at work. The nurse and she seemingly don't have a strong attraction for each other.

Sunday. November 2, 1986

Raymond calls me "mama," and "sister" (a name he called his oldest, deceased sister), especially at night. At times, he talks rationally, and speaks distinctly, and at other times, he mumbles and is not understandable. He has temper tantrums by hitting the bed or chair, or simply by just pulling on the rails. This happens if someone says or does something that he does not like. One of his brothers in Milwaukee, Wisconsin, called long distance today to check on him, and his sister visited. This seemingly relieved his mind some. He slept some while his sister was here.

He is not eating well, often refusing to eat at all. He requests "something good" to eat; yet, nothing tastes good. He often speaks intelligently. He requested his "overalls" all day. So, I finally hung them on the bed. When his sister asked what he wanted his clothes for, he said, "I need to go and vote." The election he speaks of is November 4th. He argues or disagrees in an unrecognizable statement, but you can tell that he is unhappy. His abdomen protrudes, his respirations are rapid, and he sleeps with his eyes open. You have to look closely at him to see if he is alive. I'm to ask the doctor tomorrow when I go to work about the possibility of him having a transfusion. But, I ask myself, "Is that humane?" "Should he be allowed to die in dignity?"

I'm to have a mammogram tomorrow. My left breast hurts, and a mass is present, seemingly. Is it stress, cancer, or a cyst? Doubt is in my mind. A pap smear will be done on November 11th. I guess I'm more cautious about cancer prevention now.

Also, tomorrow I'm expecting Raymond's first Social Security disability check. I received an invoice from the nursing agency that cares for him, and the amount owed them is $600.00. This will cover the month of October and the LPN caring for him. She works five days a week while I work. His Foley catheter was changed today.

Tuesday, November 4, 1986

I deposited Raymond's first Social Security benefit check. Even though he can hardly talk, he asks me about the money he received. After I showed him the deposit slip for $900.00, he felt OK about it, and said, "I just want to know where my money is going." He is to be transfused today. I have to make plans for transportation to the hospital via the ambulance. His speech is slurred. At times, he makes rational statements--even cute ones like: "Do you love me?" "Make me well," and "I hate that I'm like this." "Is the light bill paid?"

His brother, Carl, called today from Milwaukee, Wisconsin, to check on him.

Chapter Nine

HOSPITALIZATION: NOVEMBER 9-30, 1986 AND DEATH

Sunday, November 9, 1986

Raymond was admitted to the hospital again today. His temperature is 103.4° rectally. He is having severe pains, like a woman in labor. He has been asking to be admitted for two or three days. At first, the doctor said that there is no justification for admission when there is no fever. So now, he's not eating or drinking, has a fever, and uncontrollable pain. The female doctor on call asked me on admission if we wanted to be "aggressive" in the event of impending death or a sudden change for the worse.

I replied "No!" Raymond had already mentioned in the past that he wanted no life support systems used on him. Raymond told Ray, Jr. and me last night, "I love you all, but I'm tired. I'm so tired of hurting." But after getting into the hospital, and they started giving him intravenous fluids and antibiotics, along with intravenous Morphine at 5 mg.-per hour, he began to rest some. They administered Tylenol for the fever also.

At 6:35 p.m. today, he is sleeping without signs of pain or suffering. I wonder in my mind if he'll be able to go back home. He requested that Ray, Jr. and Juan come back home this weekend. He said, "It might be the last time." They gave him so much comfort this past weekend. I talked to all of them last night. I could see them sinking as I explained that the time on earth for their father might not be long. I told the two older boys to bring a dark suit if they have to come home suddenly. Kevron, the youngest, cried. Ray, Jr. said that he knew that his daddy was tired of suffering. Juan made the comment, "He's not dead yet." They all are visibly shaken.

Eddie, a brother who visited him once, maybe twice, during his two-year illness, came with Alfred, another brother, to our home today. But, Raymond had been transported by ambulance to the hospital. His sister promised to come after work, but as I write, it's 6:40 p.m. and she hasn't shown up yet. I ask myself, "Why do family members act like this during critical times?" Sometimes, seemingly very caring, and at other times, very crazy. This bothers me because it bothered Raymond so much. He shed tears, stating that they had turned their backs on him at times. This will take prayer for me to overcome.

Raymond lived in this world, was deeply loved by his parents and siblings, but, in the final hours, the children and I prevent him from being alone--no close friends even. I hope he finds solace in the "great beyond." Seemingly, the sunset today was the most beautiful I had ever seen. Kevron and I watched it from Raymond's hospital window. I told my son that it reminded me of heaven, and he remarked, "I don't want to think of other worlds at this time."

Thursday, November 13, 1986

Lord, help me is my prayer! The pump that regulates the Morphine that they are giving Raymond had to be raised up to 90. They did this when I went home. His sister stayed with him while I went home for a while. Today is the first real cold spell for this year. It is cold! Raymond's conversation is not always understood, but, usually if you listen attentively, you can make out some words.

Then, at other times, he speaks fairly distinctly. After intravenous antibiotics, intravenous fluids (Dextrose – 5% and one-half normal Saline), and intravenous Morphine, his temperature is about normal. Sometimes when you look at him, he appears to be dying, then hours later he will wake up and look good. The doctors have predicted that he will live a few days, but I doubt them. I believe I will be able to take him home again, possibly. No lab work or studies are being done per order of the oncologist. He is bathed, turned, and is given sips of liquids. We received flowers from the hospital administrator, and visits from co-workers.

The Pride Circle (Missionary Society) at the church we attend sent $72.00 this week. I called the church and reported his hospitalization. His sister has been coming in the afternoons after work, so I can go home and get Kevron. This afternoon, however, he wanted to stay home and sleep. I think seeing his father is getting to be too depressing. But, in one hour of going home, I put in a load of clothes in the washer, sold Ray, Jr.'s car for $100.00, went through the mail, and brought supper of a hamburger, french fries and a drink.

Other visitors today included Annette, my first maternal cousin, and Raymond's cousins, Dorothy Jean, Ida Bell, Sarah, and a friend, Mechee. The temperature is predicted to drop to 23º tonight, but Raymond's hospital room is comfortable--temperature wise. The Morphine pump is set at 90 (that's nine mg./hour). His respirations are labored. When the pump is cut down, he has severe pain. Morphine is known to depress the respirations. I've asked the doctors to keep him comfortable, but now it's hard to watch him. I think he might stop breathing.

Saturday, November 15, 1986

The sale of Ray, Jr.'s car was finalized today. The new owner had to visit me at the hospital to ask for the keys. I forgot to give them to him. He forgot to ask for them. My mind is so bogged down.

Raymond's Morphine pump is at 100 (10 mg./hour). You see, they mixed 25 mg. of Morphine in 250 cc. fluid. His respirations are eight per minute. When he was well, his respiratory rate was from 15 to 20 per minute.

When I arrived at the hospital today, Raymond expressed such joy to see me by smiling and saying, "Hey, Vertis." He motioned for me to come close, and he pulled on my sweater so I could kiss him. At 10:20 a.m., another doctor visited for the oncologist on the case. Raymond had been receiving intravenous fluids for feeding at 200 cc/hour, and intravenous fluid with the Morphine in it.

This is leading to overload in the system, so the doctor today had the fluid rate readjusted. The doctor was polite, and asked if there was anything he could do to help out with the situation. I asked him if he thought Raymond would ever be well enough to go home and he said that he doubts it. I expressed my frustration to him regarding the difficulty we are experiencing in suctioning Raymond. He bites on the catheter when it is introduced into his mouth, preventing us from removing the secretions from his throat. He is deteriorating right before my eyes, and I'm nervous. I'm smoking more cigarettes than I thought possible for me in an effort to relieve anxiety. Kevron keeps on at me to fill out the Readers Digest Sweepstakes entry. I think I will. This will give me diversion, as well as a possible financial boost.

Monday, November 16, 1986

At 12:40 p.m., my friend Brenda and her husband visited after church. Raymond was in a rage. By now, the acting supervisor has come in to add 50 mg. of Morphine to the present bottle, making it 100 mg. She then set the machine at 100 (10 mg./hour). At 1:15 p.m., he is asleep after moaning for six consecutive hours. I'm wondering if the pain is causing his temperature to go up. Raymond moaned and groaned during the night. At 10:00 a.m. today, the Morphine drip was set at 120 via the pump. Later, I went to the desk to ask for Valium to be given orally (dissolved in water and via sips). At 11:25 a.m., his temperature was 103º. The moans are continuous. The Morphine pump is adjusted to 125. The nurse appears nervous about giving so much Morphine, but even now, he isn't asleep.

I'm praying now to God for the right thing. Raymond has been sick for nearly two years. Now the end appears near, and I'm not ready for it. I feel alone.

Friends call me over the phone. My sister and Kevron came by and brought me dinner, but I still feel alone. Everyone is preoccupied with their lives, seemingly. I called to get my brother, Bernard, to keep Kevron a while yesterday, only to find that he's in Tuskegee, Alabama. Raymond's sister spent two hours with him while I got my hair done. She mentioned before coming, the need for her to get crepe paper for a church homecoming. So, after my hair shampoo, I immediately returned to the hospital. Later, she called back to the hospital to ask why I rushed back so quickly when she was there with her brother. She is busy with social activities, church activities, and weddings. So, I don't feel comfortable asking her or anyone else to relieve me at the hospital. I do feel appreciative of anything they do, however.

Thursday, November 19, 1986

As I visited my sick husband yesterday, gurgling and needing to be suctioned, the doctor came on routine rounds and asked me to step outside of the room so that he could talk to me. I was afraid of what he might say. I was afraid he'd tell me that Raymond was near the end of his life. Instead, in essence he told me to make or consider making arrangements for his discharge from the hospital. I guess I stayed in a state of shock most of the day. Sending a critically ill man home--what is medicine coming to in this country!

Friday, November 20, 1986

I received a call from one of the hospital nurses that worked on the Utilization Committee. She checks on the discharge plans, needs, and makes recommendations. Her call was in regard to making plans to take Raymond home or to a nursing home. There is one nursing home that handles patients getting IV fluids, and it is not far away. She said that U.S. Steel wouldn't financially handle nursing care in the home in this case. I'm so disturbed! Lord, help me! This is my constant prayer.

Sunday, November 22, 1986

I arrived at the hospital a little after 9:00 a.m. to find Raymond mouth-breathing and his mouth was very dirty and dry. It is caked up with material on his tongue. I used two packets of lemon and glycerin swabs, a towel, and a toothbrush to clean his mouth. I cleaned and cleaned, finally getting a small amount of blood and a swollen lip. So, I quit. The head nurse later commented on how much better his mouth looked. My nursing training has really helped throughout this ordeal. He groans and seems to have difficulty breathing. It seems that suctioning the secretions from his throat increases irritation and mucus. So, I suction him less but on and off I'm compelled to do so.

An LPN (practical nurse) working with him today told me that she had already given him a Tylenol suppository for his elevated temperature of 101°. His hands appear pale, like he needs blood. Later I went to the hospital cafeteria and got some pot pie and salad, and ate it in his room. A close family friend visited with me awhile. She works at the hospital too.

At 3:30 p.m., a male nurse now on duty came and told me that Raymond's blood pressure was 84/50. I responded by raising his head momentarily, and quickly thought that I had better lower his head, probably raising the blood pressure. I then repeated the 23rd Psalms to him twice, and told him that I love him. I'm so distressed, too numb to call anyone; yet, I'm alone. My sister, Gail, told me this morning that the relatives are behaving the way they do because I don't ask them to do things. I got angry and told her "that's good, let them stay out of the damn way!" It's her birthday. I hope she doesn't get too upset.

At 4:00 p.m., a friend of mine, Sally, called and asked if I needed anything. She would be coming after work. It's funny--after the nurse told me of Raymond's blood pressure, I felt hopeless and looked up, and the sun was going down behind a cloud--a beautiful sight--like God was standing and looking.

As I was getting ready to come to the hospital, a song came to mind, *Stay With Me Jesus*, popularized by the late Sam Cooke. The words, "in the dying hour, stay with me Jesus" kept coming into my mind.

Tuesday, November 24, 1986

I'm still here at the hospital from yesterday. Visitors come, even though I have a "No Visitors" sign on the door. One of Raymond's close friends and his cousin who was once

Raymond's roommate in another state visited. Church members and other friends came. When the Morphine ran out at 2:30 p.m., the LPN came to put up another bottle that was mixed by a RN. She asked the charge nurse the rate that it should go. The charge nurse replied "38 ml./hour." Instead she meant that this was bottle number 38. I heard it, and knew that an error was made, but I let it go thinking that maybe Raymond could tolerate it.

At 4:00 p.m. I turned him over and a moderate amount of stool came from his rectum. Later, he began to moan and cry. This sharp, efficient male nurse heard it and came in and put the pump at 75. Raymond's brother, Al, came at lunch time, making the comment that he hates to come to the hospital now. Suctioning Raymond, seeing the pain and the physical fatigue is getting to me too. At 4:20 p.m., Raymond's brother's mother-in-law came in the rain to pray for him. She still prays for healing. This is the first time in a long time that I began to think of healing. God is able! If He'd heal Raymond, I told Him that we would go around the country testifying, acknowledging Him, preaching or whatever He wanted us to do.

Thanksgiving Day: Friday, November 27, 1986

I spent last night at home, set the alarm clock to go off at 5:30 a.m. this morning. I called after 6:00 a.m. to get a report from the nurse I hired to stay with Raymond. This was his condition: temperature – 98.6 °, IV Morphine going at 90 cc./hour, and the other fluids going at the rate of 25 cc/hour. He is suctioned off and on as needed and turned every two hours. The children are at home, and are to clean the house. Later today, they're to have dinner at Raymond's sister's home. Mrs. Simmons, a sitter, is to stay with Raymond tonight so that the nurse can go and visit her mother.

At 2:00 p.m., the oncologist visited and advised me to go home for a while today. Raymond's temperature is 101° now rectally. I'm tired and it shows. A friend of the Jimerson family came and brought me a piece of potato pie. My sister called and told me that she cooked us a turkey. Bernard, my brother, also smoked us a turkey. Raymond's blood pressure is 90/60 and strong, also his pulse is good. I don't even know what to pray for now!

I went to the hospital administrator yesterday. I told him of my dilemma, and was assured not to worry about Raymond's discharge from the hospital until I hear from him again. But, as Raymond is allowed to stay, I don't know why I feel that I'm imposing upon the doctors and staff. I'm about ready to give up and let Raymond go home. One of his sister's close friends would be one of the nurses on the case if he went home. She is a very good nurse.

Saturday, November 28, 1986

I worked until 2:00 p.m. today--did as much as I could. Believe me, it was hard. I could have made it to the end of the shift but the children kept leaving Raymond's room and coming up to my workplace. They looked so disturbed. Then, two couples appeared for nursing assessments at the same time, and that did it. One couple had the wrong date and time. So, the secretaries helped me by telling them that the nurse had illness in the family and that their appointments would be rescheduled.

As I came down the hall to go to my husband's room, a longtime friend of the family asked if I had called Reverend Nevett, our minister. A nurse and this friend called him, and he was there in a few minutes. He prayed a fervent prayer. Raymond lives, but gasping for breath. His temperature was down to 99°, his pulse weaker and thready. I tried to call his sister, but was unable to reach her. She worked 11:00 p.m. to 7:00 a.m. last night and stopped by the hospital before going home. I understand she went to Nashville, Tennessee, to shop. I also called his brother, who talked nicely enough. He explained that he hasn't visited because he has been working until 9:00 p.m. nightly.

Gail, my sister, called and invited the boys over to eat. So, after Ray, Jr. ran errands for me, they went to eat. I'm sure this lessened their worries--just getting out of the hospital. We all left the hospital at midnight to go home.

Sunday, November 29, 1986

When I arrived at the hospital around 8:00 a.m., Raymond looked so bad. When the nurse came to check his blood pressure, it was 80/50. His respiratory rate was 18. When he takes a breath, the whole bed shakes. When I tried to clean his mouth, he clamps down so hard I can't do it. I announced to Raymond as I always do that "I'm here." I repeated the 23rd Psalms bible verse to him, then I turned him.

Back home, the kids were left with instructions of their duties. Ray, Jr. is to get groceries. Juan is to dry clothes and cook breakfast. Kevron is to help fold their clothes and put the groceries away when Ray, Jr. returns. A hired person is coming to clean the house thoroughly. Only through this kind of organization can I stay at the hospital so much and maintain a home.

Raymond's pulse is strong still, his urinary output is decreased. The night nurse irrigated the catheter and changed the drainage bag before leaving. He is having periods of apnea (no breathing), and it is very frightening. I ate breakfast in the hospital cafeteria, and talked with a kitchen helper. I needed the diversion!

Raymond's temperature is 99.6°. Bottle number 27 intravenous fluid is going as maintenance fluid to keep the IV open. Bottle number 62 of Morphine is going intravenously.

MONDAY, NOVEMBER 30, 1986

At 7:30 a.m., his sister called this morning, and her first question was, "How is Raymond?" I told her that his blood pressure dropped to 60/40 last night, but it's up to 70 (systolic) now. She said, "Well, I'd like to go to church today. Do you have anybody to relieve you?" I said, "Yes, my brother Leon said that he'd stay, and Ray, Jr. said that he'd stay." She then said, "I'll come at 1:00 o'clock and stay until the nurse comes at 11:00 p.m." She came after church and relieved me. Being a nurse, I should have known that this was it--the end is near, but I didn't. I was numb, and full of hope. I wasn't home one hour before the phone rang. Ray, Jr. answered it and said, "Mama, Auntie is on the line and she is crying." She said come back to the hospital. I screamed out, "Why did Raymond wait until I left? He is gone." I'd been with him over 29 consecutive hours, and when I turned my back and said, "I'm gone," he died. This hurt for many months to come. After this outburst, I was unable to show emotion anymore.

The funeral was three days later--a decent, dignified ceremony. There were many beautiful flowers. The soloist at the end sang, "The Best of Your Service," in an upbeat way. The minister started the eulogy by saying, "I don't know why people suffer." Raymond's sister's minister read the scriptures. He was laid to rest near my mother. My heart did ache, as did my three boys.

THINGS I'VE LEARNED FROM THESE EXPERIENCES!
THINGS I WANT YOU TO KNOW . . .

1. Cancer is devastating. It can be painful, causing many disturbances to the mind and body. Every case is individual, just as the treatment and responses.

2. Remember, "You have not, because you ask not." If you are in need of help in any way, someone will come to your aid if you ask.

3. Some people will be helpful and encouraging, while others will stand on the sideline. This includes relatives--especially relatives.

4. "Men always ought to pray." Luke 18:1 (King James version of the Holy Bible.)
   Prayer changes things.

5. The caregiver should keep dental and medical appointments to maintain good health.

6. Because you're going through a turbulent time, other life issues can and will occur. Brace yourself--some of them, unpleasant.

7. Recently while at a church function, I read these words on a bulletin board -- "Great reasons to write."
   - *a. Write to share your ideas*
   - *b. Write to explain something*
   - *c. Write to tell your side of the story*
   - *d. Write to tell what happened*
   - *e. Write to connect with your reader*
   - *f. Write to tell how you feel*
   - *g. Write to explain what you think*
   - *h. Write to remember important details*
   - *i. Write to describe something*
   - *j. Write to enjoy yourself.*

   All of the above can apply to writing of this book.

8. When going through the struggles of cancer, you have to "let go" of many challenges. This applies to the caregiver and the patient. You must continue and move forward.

9. As a caregiver, you'll become overwhelmed many times. Try to find stress releasing mechanisms. Something as simple as going on the porch or outside and taking a deep breath. When you return inside, you'll feel different.

10. Strive to decrease caregiver depression....
    (humming a song, saying a prayer, laughing with a friend, etc.)

Addendum: Lab Studies And Progress Notes

CLINICAL LABORATORIES — PERMANENT PATIENT SUMMARY REPORT

Baptist Medical Center, 701 Princeton Ave, Birmingham, AL 35211

PATIENT: JIMERSON, RAYMOND
**DISCHARGED 10/19/84
NUMBER: 273836 M 51
DOCTOR: MCLEAN, BARRY
DATE: 10/20/ 06:55
PAGE: 4
ADMITTING DIAGNOSIS: LUMBAGO

HOSPITAL DAY:	1	2	3		NORMALS	UNITS
DATE:	10/15	10/16	10/17			
ST TENDED					BLOOD	
SODIUM		142.			135.–145.	MEQ/L
POTASSIUM		4.0			3.5–5.0	MEQ/L
CHLORIDE		110. H			96.–108.	MEQ/L
CO2		28.			23.–30.	MEQ/L
BUN		9.			8.–23.	MG/DL
CREAT		1.1			0.7–1.6	MG/DL
GLUCOSE		92.			70.–110.	MG/DL
URIC AC		5.5			2.0–7.5	MG/DL
INOR P		4.0 H			1.9–3.9	MG/DL
CALCIUM		7.1 L			8.2–10.4	MG/DL
TRIGLYCR		131.			40.–200.	MG/DL
CHOL		175.			160.–310.	MG/DL
D BILI		0.1			0.0–0.2	MG/DL
T BILI		0.5			0.2–1.0	MG/DL
T PROT		6.0 L			6.8–8.0	GM/DL
GGTP		47.			8.–65.	U/L
ALK PHOS		485. H			25.–95.	U/L
SGTP-ALT		19.			10.–60.	U/L
SGOT-AST		25.			10.–45.	U/L
LDH		146.			90.–200.	U/L
CPK		51.			20.–200.	U/L
AMYLASE		64.			40.–120.	U/L
GAP		4. L			10.–18.	MMOL/L
BUN/CR		8. L			12.–20.	
OSMOL		281.			253.–306.	MOS/KG
A/G RATI		1.2			1.1–1.8	
IND BILI		0.40			0.2–0.8	MG/DL
ECTROPHOR					BLOOD	
G GLOB		1.18			0.62–1.80	GM/DL
B GLOB		0.75			0.56–1.12	GM/DL
A2 GLOB		0.59			0.32–0.73	GM/DL
A1 GLOB		0.30 H			0.08–0.26	GM/DL
ALBUMIN		3.17 L			3.55–4.99	GM/DL

*************************** MISCELLANEOUS ***************************

PHOS	(0540)				BLOOD	
RESULT	10.5 H				0.0–0.8	U/L

Addendum: Lab Studies And Progress Notes

```
Medical Center                    CLINICAL LABORATORIES                    Baptist Medical Cen
nclair Rd                     PERMANENT PATIENT SUMMARY REPORT             701 Princeton Ave
   AL 35213                                                                Birmingham, AL 35211

  IENT  JIMERSON, RAYMOND                              LOCATION    DATE  10/20/8
        **DISCHARGED 10/19/84                                            06:55
  BER      273836      M   51      DOCTOR  MCLEAN, BARRY                 PAGE    3
ADMITTING DIAGNOSIS:   LUMBAGO
OSPITAL DAY:      1         2         3
       DATE:    10/15      10/16    10/17                       NORMALS      UNITS
ST

OMBS TEST                                                       BLOOD
   DIRECT                  NEG                                  NEGATIVE

 D AGGLUT                           *1                          BLOOD
   PATIENT                1/2=+2                                <1:32        DILS
         *1  1/4=+1, 1/8=WEAK, 1/16=NEG


NE M PROF                                                       BLOOD
    PH#                   H84-1504

*********************************** CHEMISTRY *************************************

*********************************** SURVEY    *************************************

MPREHENSVE
  YROXIN                  (0540)                                BLOOD
    T4                     6.3                                  4.0-11.0     MCG/DL
```

Addendum: Lab Studies And Progress Notes

```
1st Medical Center                    CLINICAL LABORATORIES                           Baptist Medical C
                                   PERMANENT PATIENT SUMMARY REPORT                   701 Princeton Ave
                                                                                      Birmingham, Al 352
PATIENT  JIMERSON, RAYMOND
         **DISCHARGED 10/19/84                                       LOCATION              10/20/
                                                                                            06:55
NUMBER   273836       M   51           DOCTOR   MCLEAN, BARRY                        PAGE      2
ADMITTING DIAGNOSIS:   LUMBAGO
HOSPITAL DAY:       1           2           3
       DATE:     10/15       10/16       10/17
TEST                                                              NORMALS        UNITS

********************** BONE MARROW PROFILE ************************

BONE MARROW
  BLOOD COUNT       (1000)                                 BLOOD
     WBC             6.5                                    4.8-10.8         K/MM3
     RBC             3.10  L                                4.60-6.20        M/MM3
     HGB             8.6   L                                14.0-18.0        GM
     HCT            27.0   L                                42.0-52.0        %
     MCV            87.1                                    78.0-96.0        U3
     MCH            27.9                                    27.0-31.0        UUG
     MCHC           32.0                                    32.0-36.0        %
     RDW            11.6   H                                8.5-11.5
     PLT           349.0   #                                150.0-450.0      K/MM3

  DIFFERENTIAL                                             BLOOD
     BAND            3.
     SEG            76.
     LYMPH          16.
     MONO            2.
     EOSIN           3.
     PLT EST       NORM
     ANISO          SLT
     POIK           SLT
     POLY           MOD

  RETIC COUNT                                              BLOOD
     RESULT          2.1   H                                0.1-2.0          %

  PROTIME                                                  BLOOD
     CONTROL        11.3                                                     SEC
     PATIENT        11.8                                    10.5-14.0        SEC

  PTT                                                      BLOOD
     CONTROL        25.0                                                     SEC
     PATIENT        21.9                                    19.0-40.0        SEC

  IRON & TIBC                                              BLOOD
     IRON           41.    L                                70.-170.         MCG/D
     TIBC          212.    L                                270.-380.        MCG/D
     SATURATN       19.    L                                26.-45.          %
```

Addendum: Lab Studies And Progress Notes

```
Baptist Medical Center                CLINICAL LABORATORIES              Baptist Medical
                                    PERMANENT PATIENT SUMMARY REPORT     701 Princeton Av
                                                                         Birmingham, Al

PATIENT   JIMERSON, RAYMOND                                              DATE 10/2
          **DISCHARGED 10/19/84                                               06:
NUMBER    273836      M   51       DOCTOR  MCLEAN, BARRY                 PAGE
          ADMITTING DIAGNOSIS:  LUMBAGO
HOSPITAL DAY:      1        2         3
       DATE:    10/15     10/16     10/17
TEST                                                      NORMALS      UNI

************************************ HEMATOLOGY **********************************

BLOOD COUNT             (0540)                            BLOOD
   WBC                    6.7                             4.8-10.8      K/M
   RBC                    2.76 L                          4.60-6.20     M/M
   HGB                    7.9  L                          14.0-18.0     GM
   HCT                   24.0  L                          42.0-52.0     %
   MCV                   86.8                             78.0-96.0     U3
   MCH                   28.7                             27.0-31.0     UUG
   MCHC                  33.1                             32.0-36.0     %
   RDW                   11.9  H                          8.5-11.5
   PLT                  304.0                             150.0-450.0   K/M

DIFFERENTIAL            (0540)                            BLOOD
   BAND                   6.
   SEG                   66.
   LYMPH                 20.
   MONO                   3.
   EOSIN                  5.
   PLT EST              NORM
   ANISO                 SLT
   POIK                  SLT
   POLY                  SLT

                                              ------ URINALYSIS ------

URINALYSIS             ( PM )                             URINE
   COLOR              YELLOW
   TURBID              CLEAR
   SP GRAV             1.010
   PH                    7.0
   PROTEIN              NEG.
   GLUCOSE              NEG.
   KETONES              NEG.
   BILE                 NEG.
   BLOOD                NEG.
   WBC'S                 0-2                                             /HP
   EPI CELL              0-2                                             /HP
```

Addendum: Lab Studies And Progress Notes

Baptist Medical Centers
X-RAY REQUISITION

X-Ray No. 1984 OCT 17 Tech: NB   10/19   DATE 10-17-84

Radiologist: BE 10/18

RADIOLOGIC EXAMINATION OF: IVP "wt loss, anemia"

X-Ray Service Code: 1264415

Clinical Diagnosis & Remarks: Lumbago

Service of Dr. McLean   Nurse: LS

RADIOLOGIC AND FLUOROSCOPIC FINDINGS

10-18-84

IVP: Scout film reveals a mottled appearance to the bony pelvis, consistent with metastatic disease as previously described.

Following injection of the contrast, there is bilateral excretion noted at 5 minutes. Renal contours and intrarenal collecting systems are normal in appearance. The left ureter appears normal. The most distal portion of the right ureter is dilated, and this is suspicious for ureterocele. There is no evidence of obstruction. The distal third of the right ureter is deviated medially, and this is suspicious for pelvis adenopathy. The bladder is not adequately filled for evaluation. The patient voided well.

OPINION:
Possible right ureterocele. Medial deviation of the right ureter, please see above comments. Normal upper tracts. Bony metastasis.

B. EMBRY, M.D./jl
MM

Addendum: Lab Studies And Progress Notes

HISTORY AND PHYSICAL

Page 2

Name: JIMERSON, RAYMOND   Room No: 692-B   Unit No: 273836-A

Date of Admission: 10/15/84   Attending Physician: Dr. Barry McLean
                                                    Dr. S. Real

Date of Discharge: / /

Past lab work in the clinic includes bone x-rays, which showed lytic and blastic lesions in the patient's skull and a bone scan that has multiple hot spots throughout his bones.

IMPRESSION: 1. PROBABLE CARCINOMA, THE MOST PROBABLE CAUSE BEING MULTIPLE MYELOMA OR PROSTATE CANCER.

PLAN: 1. Bone marrow biopsy.
        2. Serum acid phosphatase level.
        3. Further work up for probable carcinoma.

SR/jg
Dictated 10/16/84
Transcribed 10/17/84

† The Cross And Weeping Still †

Addendum: Lab Studies And Progress Notes

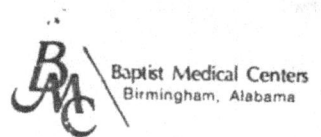

HISTORY AND PHYSICAL

Page 1

Name: JIMERSON, RAYMOND   Room No: 692-B   Unit No: 273836-A

Date of Admission: 10/15/84   Attending Physician: Dr. Barry McLean
                                                    Dr. S. Real
Date of Discharge: / /

PRESENT ILLNESS: Mr. Jimerson is a 51 year old black male, who for the past several months has been feeling tired, having night sweats, has had a 25 pound weight loss and was told by another doctor that his blood count was real low and he has been having pain in numerous areas of his bone, particularly his lower back. The patient attributed all of these problems to his hemorrhoids, which were fixed approximately two months ago. However since he continued to have problems even after the hemorrhoids were fixed, he continued to seek medical attention. The patient denies any cough, cold, fevers, nausea, vomiting, diarrhea, constipation, hematuria or hematochezia since his hemorrhoids were fixed.

PAST MEDICAL HISTORY: Positive for hemorrhoids, which were fixed approximately two months ago. Seven years ago the patient had a TUR-P for an enlarged prostate. Otherwise the patient has been healthy. The patient is not allergic to any medications but he gets nauseated on Codeine compounds. He is currently taking no medications.

FAMILY HISTORY: Positive for heart disease, hypertension and stroke. He has also had one sister, who had a GI carcinoma.

SOCIAL HISTORY: The patient does not smoke or drink. He lives here in Birmingham. He works as a guard over at U. S. Steel.

REVIEW OF SYSTEMS: Noncontributory.

PHYSICAL EXAMINATION

GENERAL: The patient is a 51 year old black male, well developed in no apparent distress.
VITAL SIGNS: Blood pressure 120/84. He is afebrile. His pulse is 80 and his respirations are 16.
HEENT: Pupils are equal, round and reactive to light and accomodation. Extraocular eye muscles are intact. Fundi; the disks are sharp and the TMs are clear. Mouth; tongue and uvula midline.
NECK: Supple. No adenopathy and no carotid bruits heard and no thyromegaly.
LUNGS: Clear.
HEART: Regular rate and rhythm without murmur, rub or gallop.
ABDOMEN: Soft and nontender. Bowel sounds are positive. There is no organomegaly. No CVAT. He does have mild tenderness in the lower lumbar area aspect of his back to palpation.
EXTREMITIES: No clubbing, cyanosis or edema.
GU: Normal male.
RECTAL: Mildly enlarged prostate. No nodules or firm places noted. Guaiac negative.
NEURO: Cranial nerves II-XII are intact. Motor and sensory are grossly intact. DTRs are 2+ and symmetric. No cerebellar signs. Gait is normal.

Addendum: Lab Studies And Progress Notes

DISCHARGE SUMMARY

Page 1   CC: Dr. R. Navari

Name: JIMERSON, RAYMOND   Room No: 692-B   Unit No: 273836-A

Date of Admission: 10/15/84   Attending Physician: Dr. Barry McLean
                                                    Dr. S. Real
Date of Discharge: 10/19/84

The patient is a 51 year old black male, who for the past several months has been feeling tired, having night sweats. Has had a 25 pound weight loss and was told by another doctor that his blood count was very low. The patient has also been complaining of pain in numerous areas, particularly in his low back. The patient attributed all of these problems to his hemorrhoids, which were fixed approimately two months ago. However since he has continued to have problems after the hemorrhoids were fixed, he decided to seek medical attention. The patient's studies included a hematocrit of 24%. Bone scan showed extensive metastatic disease. Plain films of rib and pelvic region showed multiple mixed lytic and blastic lesions. A liver spleen scan was normal. During the hospitalization the diagnostic studies consisted of a bone marrow aspiration of both the right and left anterior superior iliac crest. These both came back with metastatic adenocarcinoma, which was compatible with prostatic origin. The patient also had an acid phosphatase, which was 10.5. His hematocrit on admission was 24%. The patient also had an IVP, which was normal. Bone marrow and acid phosphatase gave us a diagnosis of prostatic cancer and Dr. Rudy Navari was consulted for treatment of his cancer with extensive metastases. The patient was started on DES treatments following radiation therapy to his breasts. The patient is to be seen in follow up by Dr. Navari in approximately two weeks.

SR/jg
Dictated 10/19/84
Transcribed 10/22/84

Addendum: Lab Studies And Progress Notes

LLOYD NOLAND CLINIC RECORD

UROLOGY CLINIC
AUG 0 8 1978

Raymond's IVP was normal. We cystoscoped him today. He does have some rather significant obstruction of the bladder neck area contracture. We will plan to admit him to the hospital on 8/13 and resect bladder neck on the 15th. He has already had an IVP so this does not need to be repeated.

Walter G. Pittman, M.D./mc

UROLOGY CLINIC
SEP 0 1 1978

Raymond recently had a TUR of the bladder neck in prostate. His post-operative course was benign. He is doing well at this point. Urine specimen is relatively clear. He can be discharged from GU Clinic and return to work six weeks from time of surgery.

Walter G. Pittman, M.D./mc

UROLOGY CLINIC
SEP 2 1978

Raymond continues to do well. His urine is clear and he is having no difficulties at this time. He can be discharged.

Walter G. Pittman, M.D./sj

Addendum: Lab Studies And Progress Notes

LLOYD NOLAND HOSPITAL

1-C REVISED 6-78

D: 10-4-78   Admitted 8-10-78, Discharged 8-20-78

FINAL DIAGNOSIS: Benign prostatic hypertrophy

This was a 46 year old black male who presented with a six months history of pressure sensation on urinating especially in the evenings. He was seen in the GU clinic and was found to have bladder neck obstruction. On admission he was in no acute distress. His blood pressure was 130/90, pulse 65. Pulmonary status was within normal limits.

The patient was taken to the operating room and transurethral resection of the prostate was done under spinal anesthesia which he tolerated well.

LABORATORY DATA: WBC on admission was 5,600. Hemoglobin 12.9, hematocrit 38.4. Urinalysis was negative. Acid phos. 1.2. Urine cultures were negative. SMA 6 and 12 were within normal limits except for triglyceride level of 368. Chest x-ray was normal.

HOSPITAL COURSE: The patient's hospital and postoperative course was uneventful. He was maintained on Demerol and Vistaril q 4 h for pain and Dalmane for sleep. Later was placed on Tylenol #3. His Foley catheter was removed and he voided without trouble.

He was discharged, his condition improved to be followed up in the GU clinic.

F. J. BELL, M.D.

FJB/sg
T: 10-6-78

LAST NAME OF PATIENT: JIMERSON   FIRST: RAYMOND SR   BED OR ROOM NO: 3B 353   PATIENT CHART NUMBER: 08 68 02 S

ADMISSION NO. 92828

Addendum: Lab Studies And Progress Notes

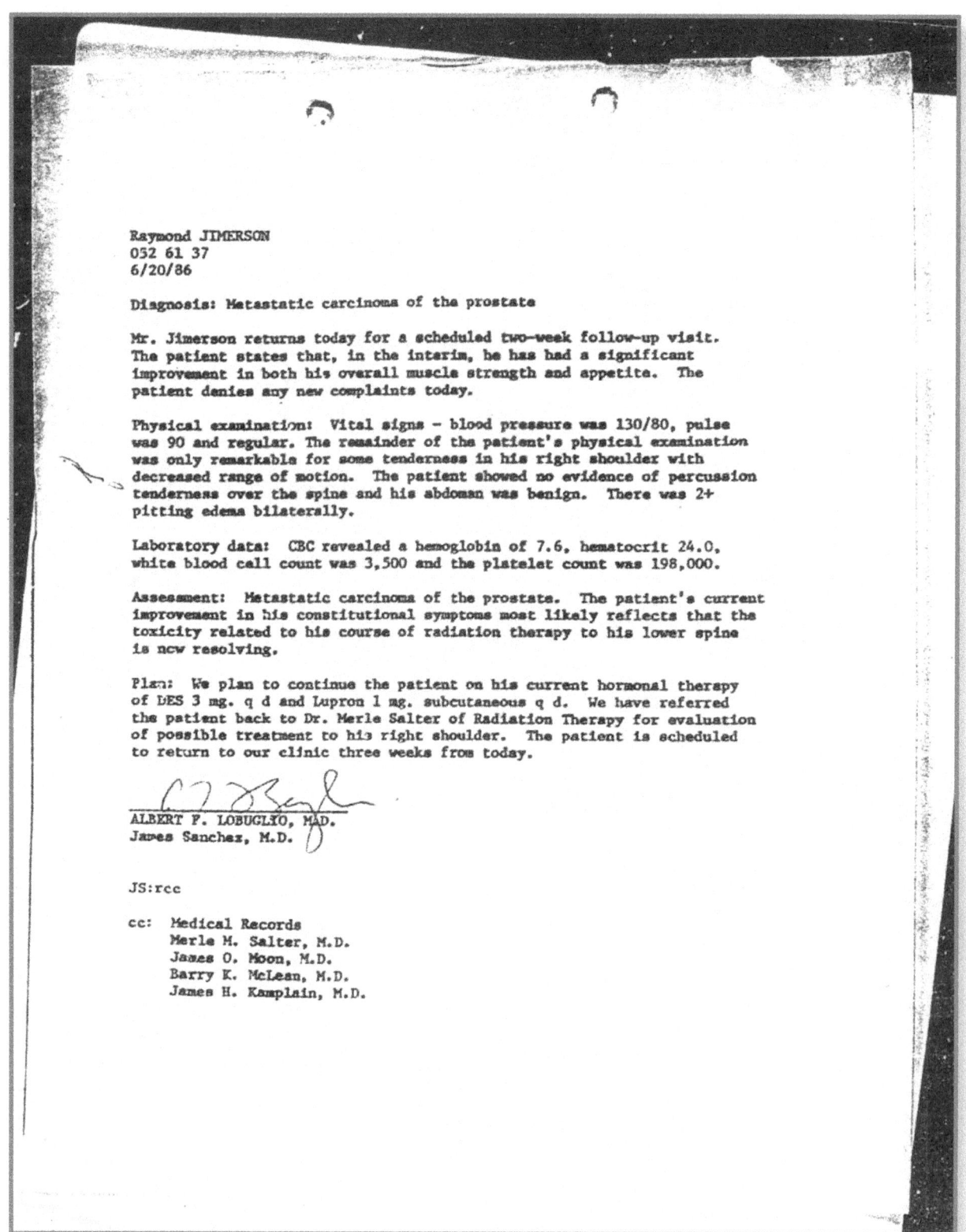

Raymond JIMERSON
052 61 37
6/20/86

Diagnosis: Metastatic carcinoma of the prostate

Mr. Jimerson returns today for a scheduled two-week follow-up visit. The patient states that, in the interim, he has had a significant improvement in both his overall muscle strength and appetite. The patient denies any new complaints today.

Physical examination: Vital signs - blood pressure was 130/80, pulse was 90 and regular. The remainder of the patient's physical examination was only remarkable for some tenderness in his right shoulder with decreased range of motion. The patient showed no evidence of percussion tenderness over the spine and his abdomen was benign. There was 2+ pitting edema bilaterally.

Laboratory data: CBC revealed a hemoglobin of 7.6, hematocrit 24.0, white blood cell count was 3,500 and the platelet count was 198,000.

Assessment: Metastatic carcinoma of the prostate. The patient's current improvement in his constitutional symptoms most likely reflects that the toxicity related to his course of radiation therapy to his lower spine is now resolving.

Plan: We plan to continue the patient on his current hormonal therapy of DES 3 mg. q d and Lupron 1 mg. subcutaneous q d. We have referred the patient back to Dr. Merle Salter of Radiation Therapy for evaluation of possible treatment to his right shoulder. The patient is scheduled to return to our clinic three weeks from today.

ALBERT F. LOBUGLIO, M.D.
James Sanchez, M.D.

JS:rcc

cc: Medical Records
    Merle M. Salter, M.D.
    James O. Moon, M.D.
    Barry K. McLean, M.D.
    James H. Kamplain, M.D.

Addendum: Lab Studies And Progress Notes

the University of Alabama in Birmingham
the Medical Center / UNIVERSITY OF ALABAMA HOSPITALS

HISTORY, PHYSICAL EXAMINATION AND PROGRESS NOTES

NOTES

SH - ⊕ US Steel work × 19 years applying for disability
ROS - ⊕ Anemia × several months - 2° bone involvement
⊕ DOE 2° Anemia
∅ Chest pain h/o cardiac failure MI ect

PE: Gen WDWN BM wearing condom catheter
Afebrile HR 80 BP 130/70 RR 16
HEENT - PERRL EOMI Fundi - benign OP clean
NCAT
neck - supple ∅ N Bruits Masses
CV - RRR ∅ M G R nl S₁ S₂
lungs - BBS clear
abd - sl obese sft NT NDS BS⊕
gu - BCCAT sl ↓ anal sphincter tone
MS - ∅ paraspinal tenderness ⊕ L UE pain c̄ ROM
⊕ R hip pain c̄ ROM
ext - ∅ c/k/e
neuro - CN 2-12 intact
MS - A+O×3 Affect appropriate
sensory - pinprick proprioception intact
motor - 5/5 all ext
cerebellar - nl F to N H to shin difficult to
assess L UE 2° MS pain
Babinski ↓ L

FORM N-12 REV. 6-64 PAGE 2

Addendum: Lab Studies And Progress Notes

the University of Alabama in Birmingham
the Medical Center / UNIVERSITY OF ALABAMA HOSPITALS

HISTORY, PHYSICAL EXAMINATION AND PROGRESS NOTES

AI - H+P - On call

5:30 PM Source - Pt + clinic notes. Old chart not available

CC: loss of bowel and bladder control

HPI - This 54 y/o BM c̄ stage D Prostatic CA presents c̄ gradual loss of bowel + bladder control. Approx 2y PTA pt presented c̄ lumbosacral pain ⊕ Bone scan for lumbosacral mets + TURP bx ⊕ for prostatic CA. DES x 2 years. H/O RT to LS spine + ® hip. F/U on 3/86 showed bony mets on scan to ribs, femur, thoracic + lumbar spine, humerus + pelvis. Acid ø(2/86) ≈ 17.21. Alk ø - 416. Hgb/Hct ≈ 7.9/25.4. ⊕ c/o ® ® shoulder pain x 1 month (x® humeral mets). ⊕ ® hip pain c̄ ® ® LE weakness x 1 month. ⊕ gradual loss of "tight" anal sphincter control x 1 month. ⊕ gradual progressive loss of urinary sphincter control x 4-5 days. Loss of anal sphincter tone when seen by Dr. Moon today. Admitted at recommendation of Dr. Shaw from Dr. Lubushio's clinic.

PMHx - TURP - 1980
Meds - DES 3mg po QD
       Lupron 1.0mg SQ QD
NDKA
FH - mother - d/ gallbladder CA
     sister d/ colon CA
     father d/ - gunshot wound

FORM N-12 REV. 6-64 PAGE 2

Addendum: Lab Studies And Progress Notes

the University of Alabama in Birmingham
the Medical Center / UNIVERSITY OF ALABAMA HOSPITALS

HISTORY, PHYSICAL EXAMINATION AND PROGRESS NOTES   Jimmerson, Raymond

6/6/86   NOTES   0526137

Mr. Jimmerson returns after a several week time interval.

He has gotten some minimal relief from his pain but not anything really marked.

He is complaining of some cervical spine pain. We have taken a film which shows

no evidence of gross metastatic disease. His pain should be better controlled by

meds and I have given him a prescription for tylenol 3, darvacet. We will withhold

any further radiation at this time.

Merle M. Salter, M.D./kfb

cc: Medical Records Dept.

Dr. Donald Miller

Addendum: Lab Studies And Progress Notes

Raymond JIMERSON
052 61 37
6/6/86

Diagnosis: Metastatic prostate carcinoma

Mr. Jimerson returns to clinic today feeling about the same as before with chronic fatigue as his major complaint. He has no notable exertional dyspnea but states that he has voluntarily decreased his exercise. His physical examination today is unchanged.

His hematocrit is 22.6, hemoglobin 7.3 with a white blood cell count of 3,500 and a platelet count of 218,000. This represents a significant drop in his hematocrit from 30.6 to 22.6 over the last two weeks. Because of his continuing anemia, we are quite concerned that he is not having a good response to the combined DES and Lupron therapy. However, because he had extensive radiation therapy recently involving the left shoulder and the spine from C7 to S1, this marrow suppression due to radiation therapy may be also contributing to his anemia. Therefore, we have elected to continue Lupron 1 mg. and DES 3 mg. per day and we will follow him along. We arranged to have him get three units of packed red blood cells by transfusion on 6/9/86 and we will see him back in approximately two weeks for re-evaluation. It may be necessary to start him on chemotherapy soon, and we feel that the best regimen will probably be Adriamycin 20 mg./m^2 intravenously weekly. This should be relatively well tolerated and we can keep a close watch on his marginal hematocrit and white blood cell count.

ALBERT F. LOBUGLIO, M.D.
George M. Shaw, M.D.

GMS:rcc

cc: Medical Records
    Barry K. McLean, M.D.
    James H. Kamplain, M.D.

Addendum: Lab Studies And Progress Notes

Raymond JIMERSON
052 61 37
5/23/86

Diagnosis: Metastatic prostate carcinoma

Mr. Jimerson returns to the clinic having been discharged from the hospital on 5/14/86. He was admitted because of apparent spinal chord impingement based on physical examination and an LS myelogram showed diffuse metastasis with extra-dural axial compression from tumor in the lower thoracic spine region. He subsequently underwent radiation therapy to the spine from C7 to S1 which was completed today. He also received radiation therapy to the left shoulder for metastatic disease. Throughout this time, he has continued on Lupron 1 mg. subcutaneously daily as well as DES 3 mg. a day. He feels that overall his strength and stamina is worse now than it was three months ago but relatively stable. It is difficult to assess his response to the addition of Lupron at the present time and, therefore, we have elected to continue this drug at 1 mg. subcutaneously a day along with DES at the same 3 mg. per day dose and we will see him again in two weeks. Today, his hematocrit is 30.6 up from 28 on 5/7/86.

ALBERT F. LOBUGLIO, M.D.
George M. Shaw, M.D.

GMS:rcc

cc: Medical Records
    Barry K. McLean, M.D.
    James H. Kamplain, M.D.

Addendum: Lab Studies And Progress Notes

```
MILLER    DONALD    M    UNIVERSITY OF ALABAMA HOSPITALS                              1900    1961
                              LAB RESULTS
                                 FOR
TEST              ROOM #           PATIENT NAME      MEDICAL RECORDS #   DATE      PAGE    TECH
DATE   83407  M N 054Y  W916 -30   JIMERSON-RAYM     0526137             05-24-86  002     NO.

         TIME                      WBC/CMM  POLYS%  LYMPH%  LG MONO%  RBC/CMM  XANTHO
05-07-86 1630  CELL CT/DIFF CSF       0                                   0       1+     018
               TUBE #3

         TIME   GLUC CSF  PROTEIN CSF  CHLOR CSF  BILI CSF   GLUC FLUID
                MG/DL     MG/DL        MEQ/L      MG/DL      MG/DL
05-07-86 1630   76        80                                                             059

         TIME   R P R    TREPONEMA       VDRL
                         PALLIDUM HA     CSF
05-07-86 0700   NEG                                                                      804
05-07-86 1630                                                                            804
VDRL CSF        QNS FOR TESTING

                           PATIENT   DONOR    UNIT    AMOUNT   CROSSMATCH
                           ABO RH    ABO RH   NO      GIVEN    SAL  ALB  AHG
05-05-86 0817 RED BLOOD CELLS  A POS  A POS   019839   250     NEG  NEG  NEG             068
05-05-86 1054 RED BLOOD CELLS  A POS  A POS   018577   250     NEG  NEG  NEG             068
05-05-86 1327 RED BLOOD CELLS  A POS  A POS   019386   250     NEG  NEG  NEG             068

        83407   LAST SHEET OF PATIENT RECORD.
```

Addendum: Lab Studies And Progress Notes

```
MILLER    DONALD   M        UNIVERSITY OF ALABAMA HOSPITALS              1900    1960
                                    LAB RESULTS
                                        FOR
TEST              ROOM #         PATIENT NAME    MEDICAL RECORDS #  DATE     PAGE    TECH
DATE   83407  M N 054Y  W916  30    JIMERSON-RAYM    0526137     05-24-86  001      NO.

05-07-86  05-08-86  009824  CSF CULTURE                                            008
                            NO BACTERIA SEEN ON DIRECT GRAM STAIN.
                            NEGATIVE  5 DAYS

          TIME    SODIUM    POTASSIUM   CHLORIDE   CO2 CONTENT  ANION GAP  OSMOLALITY
                  MEQ/L     MEQ/L       MEQ/L      MEQ/L                   MOSMOL
05-07-86  0700    138       4.3         105        26                                033

          TIME    GLUCOSE   UREA        CREATININE  UREA/CREAT  URIC ACID
                  MG/DL     MG/DL       MG/DL                   MG/DL
05-07-86  0700    120       7           0.8                     5.0                  033

          TIME    CALCIUM   TOT PROTEIN  CORRECTED   PHOSPHORUS  ACID PHOS  MAGNESIUM
                  MG/DL     GM/DL        CA MG/DL    MG/DL       IU/L       MG/DL
05-07-86  0700    8.6       5.9                      1.9                             033

          TIME                TOT PROT  ALBUMIN  ALPHA 1  ALPHA 2  BETA   GAMMA
                              GM/DL     GM/DL    GM/DL    GM/DL    GM/DL  GM/DL
05-07-86  0700  PROT ELECT FRACT  5.90  2.59     0.41     0.99     0.83   1.07       080

          TIME    T BILIRUB  D BILIRUB  I BILIRUB
                  MG/DL      MG/DL      MG/DL
05-07-86  0700    0.4        0.1        0.3                                          033

          TIME    LDH        GOT        LDH/GOT    CPK         GGT        ALK PHOS
                  IU/L       IU/L                  IU/L        IU/L       IU/L
05-07-86  0700    276        13                    12          122        490        033

  RBC PROFILE                                          (0-4+) H   A  AC  PC   P  P  S
                                                             M  N  Y   N  NH  OH   O  L  T
          TIME RBC/CMM  HGB   PCV   MCV     MCH    MCHC     I  A  P   I  IR  LR   I  A  I
               MILLION  GM%   %     CU-MIC  MCMCG   %       C  C  O   S  SO  YO   K  T  P
05-07-86  0700  3.12    9.8   28    91      31      35                                A      082

  WBC AND DIFF   W    L    M    S    B    E    B    M    M    O  P  B   AL   N   DB  TG
                 B    Y    O    E    A    O    A    E    Y    T  R  L   TY   UR  OO  OR
          TIME   C    M    N    G    N    S    S    T    E    H  O  A   YM   CB  HD  XA
                 CMM  P%   O%   %    D%   %    D%   A%   L%   %  %  S%  P    C   Y   N
05-07-86  0700   4500 11   11   70   04   04                                                 082

          TIME   PLATELET   PROTHROM   PROTHROM   PROTHROM    P T T        P T T
                 /CMM       CONT SEC   PAT SEC    % ACT       CONT SEC     PAT SEC
05-07-86  0700   266000     12.8       12.0       100.0       27           29                082
```

† The Cross And Weeping Still †

Addendum: Lab Studies And Progress Notes

```
UAB                    DEPARTMENT OF RADIOLOGY REPORT              05/10/86 16:34
The University of Alabama at Birmingham

       NAME   JIMERSON, RAYMOND *        DOB      12/29/31       CASE NO.   8340786126
        MRN   0526137                AGE/SEX      054Y/M          SVC/CP    30/80
   LOCATION   E9NW/W916                                          ADMITTED   05/06/86
   LOG DATE   05/10/86                LOG TIME    16:34           LOG I.D.  01
ORDER #/EXAM  0051082  SPINE LUMBOSACRAL AP&L     72100         PROC. CODE  3050 72100
  REF. PHYS.
    ADDRESS
  ORD. PHYS.  MILLER     DONALD     M         ATT. PHYS.  MILLER     DONALD     M
? TO BE ANSWERED  EVALUTE IN PT WITH PROSTATIC CA AND URINARY RETENT
                  ION.
    HISTORY   PT ADMITTED WITH PROSTATIC CA.
PRIN. DIAGNOSIS  DIAGNOSIS NOT CODED
```

LUMBOSACRAL SPINE, AP AND LATERAL, 5-10-86

Overall spin al alignment and intervertebral disc spaces are maintained. There is slight compression deformity of the L4 vertebral body with hypertrophic change. All of the vertebral bodies demonstrate mottled density, compatible with metastases. The sacrum and ilia and proximal head of the femur also show mottled and irregular density indicating diffuse metastatic involvement. The right SI joint shows metastatic involvement in the mid portion otherwise SI joints are normal.

5-11-68ek/K. BEIL, MD   B. SOTO, MD743

Transcribed By _____ Personally Rendered By _____
                                                    (Radiologist)
Resident _____
                                        TECH ID: PATRICIA LESTER, #7
                                                 LEIGH ANN HEARN

Addendum: Lab Studies And Progress Notes

```
UAB                    DEPARTMENT OF RADIOLOGY REPORT              05/07/86 15:53
The University of Alabama at Birmingham

        NAME    JIMERSON, RAYMOND *      DOB       12/29/31    CASE NO.   8340786126
        MRN     0526137                  AGE/SEX   054Y/M      SVC/CP     30/80
        LOCATION E9NE/W                                        ADMITTED   05/06/86
        LOG DATE 05/07/86                LOG TIME  15:53       LOG I.D.   01
        ORDER #/EXAM 0050019 MYELOGM LUMBOSACRAL    72266      PROC. CODE 3050 72266
        REF. PHYS.
        ADDRESS
        ORD. PHYS.    MILLER    DONALD   M         ATT. PHYS. MILLER   DONALD   M
      ? TO BE ANSWERED  PT WITH METATASTIC PROSTATE CA WITH URINARY INCONT
                        INENCE ? CAUDA SYNDROME
        HISTORY         PROSTATE CA
        PRIN. DIAGNOSIS DIAGNOSIS NOT CODED

        THORACOLUMBAR ISOVUE MYELOGRAM, 5/7/86

        HISTORY: Prostate carcinoma with recent bowel and bladder incontinence.

        TECHNIQUE: 14cc of Isovue 200 were injected into the subarachnoid
        space at L3-4, without complication. 1cc of clear, colorless CSF
        was removed and returned to the patient's ward for laboratory tests.

        FINDINGS: There are diffuse lytic metastases of T9 through T12,
        involving the pedicles of T10 through T12, and there is severe
        T9 vertebral body compression fracture. There is diffuse extradural
        compression deformity from metastases from T9 through T12. The
        upper and lower levels of metastases and extradural compression
        were marked on the anterior skin surface. There are mild anterior
        extradural defects at L3-4, L4-5 and L5-S1, with nerve root thickening
        of L5 and S1 bilaterally, almost certainly due to degenerative
        disc disease. There is no evidence of metastasis in the lumbar
        spine. Scout films demonstrate diffuse metastases in the pelvis.

        IMPRESSION: (1) Diffuse metastases from T9 through T12, with extra-axial
        compression from tumor. (2) Mild degenerative disc disease at
        L3 through S1 as discussed.



        5/8/86dw                              J. VITEK, MD/693
        R. LAWDAHL, MD




        Transcribed By _____   Personally Rendered By _____
                                                                 (Radiologist)
        Resident _____
                                          TECH ID: CYNTHIA HICKS
                                                   CRAIG WILLIAMSON
```

Addendum: Lab Studies And Progress Notes

JIMERSON, Raymond
5/6/86
052 61 37

DIAGNOSIS: Metastatic prostatic carcinoma.

Mr. Jimerson is being seen today as an unscheduled clinic visit. He received 3 units of packed red cells yesterday and states that his fatigue and decreased exercise tolerance is improved somewhat. However, over the last several days, he has lost continence of urine and has consulted his urologist, Dr. James O. Moon at Lloyd Noland Hospital. A cystoscopy apparently showed that he had markedly decreased tone of the external bladder sphincter but no masses in the bladder, in the prostate, or by rectal examination. Also, it was found that he had decreased sphincter tone on rectal examination. The patient also complained of slight numbness around the right buttock area. He denied incontinence of stool but felt that his rectal competence was not as good as it was a month ago.

On physical examination, he appeared in his usual state of health. Vital signs were normal. Head and neck examination, lungs, and heart examination were all unremarkable. Abdominal examination showed no masses and no bladder distension. Neurologic examination showed intact cranial nerves 2-12, intract motor strength in the lower extremities (patient was able to walk on his toes and on his heels), and intact sensation to vibration, light touch, and pin prick in the lower extremities. Deep tendon reflexes were 2+ in both knees. Rectal tone was decreased as was the anal wink. Given his history of recent onset bladder incontinence and decreased rectal tone, I have arranged for Mr. Jimerson to be admitted to the In-patient Oncology Service for an MRI and CT scan of the pelvis and a myelogram.

George M. Shaw, M.D.

GMS/swg

cc: Medical Records
    Barry K. McLean, M.D.
    James H. Kamplain, M.D.

Addendum: Lab Studies And Progress Notes

The University of Alabama at Birmingham   PAGE 1

The Medical Center/University of Alabama Hospital

                              DISCHARGE SUMMARY

NAME: JIMERSON, RAYMOND   MED.REC.NO. 0526137   ROOM: W916

DOCTOR/SERV.: Dr. Donald Miller/1603   ADMITTED: 5/6/86   DISCHARGED: 5/14/86

                                         DICTATED: 5/17/86   TRANSCRIBED: 5/20/86

PRIMARY DIAGNOSIS: Adenocarcinoma of the prostate with bony metastasis
                         and new onset of urinary incontinence.

PRIMARY PROCEDURE: Myelogram.
                         Radiationa therapy.
                         Cystometrogram.

DISCHARGE MEDICATIONS: Lupron 1.0 mg. subq. q.a.m., DES. 3 mg. p.o. q.d.

DISPOSITION: The patient is discharged to home with follow-up in
                         Dr. LoBuglio's clinic in two weeks. He is to
                         complete radiation therapy as an outpatient.

HISTORY OF PRESENT ILLNESS: This is a 54 year old black male who was admitted for workup of urinary incontinence. The patient was found to have metastatic adenocarcinoma of the prostate in 10/84 during workup of lower back pain. He was initially treated with DES. He later received local radiation to the L1-L5 area and left hemipelvis for intractable pain. His DES was increased to 4 mg. with nearly complete resolution of his bone pain. He referred himself to Dr. LoBuglio's clinic in 2/86 for follow-up. Acid phosphatase in 2/86 was 17. Bone scan revealed increased uptake in the ribs, femur, thoracic and lumbar vertebrae, humerus and pelvis. Plain films revealed involvement for vertebrae, pelvis, and femurs. The patient was continued on DES, now at 3 mg., until 4/18/86 when he noted new right hip pain. The patient was started on Lupron 1 mg. subq. q.d. Five days prior to admission, the patient noted urinary incontinence. He had been treated two weeks earlier with Bactrim for urinary retention. The patient was then started on Macrodantin. The patient was seen by Dr. James Moon at Lloyd Nolan and underwent cystoscopy which showed no mucosal abnormalities. The internal sphincter tone was decreased. Rectal tone was also decreased. The patient was referred for further workup. He notes a tingling sensation over the buttocks.

PAST MEDICAL HISTORY: 1) TURP in 1980, reported to show no malignancy. 2) History of anemia with a packed cell volume of 21.2. The patient was given three units of packed red blood cells. Medications: DES 1 mg. p.o. t.i.d., Lupron 1 mg. subq. q.d., Darvocet-100 two q. 4 p.r.n. No known drug allergies → *Motrin → anaphylaxis*

FAMILY HISTORY: Unremarkable.

Addendum: Lab Studies And Progress Notes

the University of Alabama in Birmingham
the Medical Center / UNIVERSITY OF ALABAMA HOSPITALS

HISTORY, PHYSICAL EXAMINATION AND PROGRESS NOTES

NOTES

Lab: 5/2/86 ICU-21 WBC - 3800 Plt 281,000
     Before 3 units PRBC Acid Ø 4/18 28.38
     Admission profile pending

EKG - NSR no acute ST∆ WNS occ unifocal PVC

CXR - pending

Old Chart - where is it?

Imp/Plan
  1. New onset incontinence - R/O spinal cord compression - myelogram in AM
  2. Prostatic CA - Apparently progressive D2 - need to see old chart
  3. Anemia - 2nd #2 - maybe but must √ old chart
  4. ↓ WBC - 2nd bony involvement? - Old chart
  5. (L) shoulder pain - 2nd bony mets
  6. (R) hip pain - 2nd femur mets

M Hayden MD

Addendum: Lab Studies And Progress Notes

Raymond JIMERSON
052 61 37
3/21/86

Diagnosis: Metastatic prostatic carcinoma

Mr. Jimerson returns for follow-up. He had a bone scan done earlier today which showed widespread uptake in the ribs, femur, thoracic and lumbar vertebra, humerus and pelvis. He also had a chest x-ray and bilateral hip films. These x-rays showed involvement of the vertebra, pelvis, and femurs with metastatic prostate carcinoma. An acid phosphatase done one month ago here at our clinic revealed a level of 17.21. Alkaline phosphatase simultaneously was 416. Hemoglobin and hematocrit at that time were 7.9 and 25.4 respectively.

At the present time, the patient is relatively asymptomatic although he has a mild amount of mid thoracic vertebral aching and some right knee pain. Because he is relatively asymptomatic and is currently taking an appropriate drug regimen for this disease (DES 3 mg. per day), we have elected to simply follow him along on a monthly basis. Should he show evidence of disease progression, at that time institution of an alternative form of therapy would be considered.

ALBERT F. LOBUGLIO, M.D.
George M. Shaw, M.D.

GMS:rcc

cc: Medical Records
   Barry K. McLean, M.D.
   James H. Kamplain, M.D.

Addendum: Lab Studies And Progress Notes

The University of Alabama at Birmingham   PAGE 2

The Medical Center/University of Alabama Hospital

DISCHARGE SUMMARY

NAME: JIMERSON, RAYMOND   MED.REC.NO. 0526137   ROOM: 1530

from C3-4-5, T3 and T9. He was admitted to the oncology service for stabilization of his spine and for evaluation by radiation oncology.

PHYSICAL EXAMINATION: He was awake, alert and oriented x three; right hand appropriate effect. Cranial nerves were completely intact. Sensory was intact to pinprick. Motor 5/5 throughout except for left deltoid which was 4/5; left biceps 4/5; rectal tone 4/5; DTR's 1+ biceps, 2+ brachials, 1+ triceps, 1+ knee jerk and 0 ankle jerk. Toes were downgoing. Cerebellar was normal.

IMPRESSION: C4-5 nerve root compression with compression fractures of C3-5.

HOSPITAL COURSE: The patient was evaluated by neurosurgery and underwent posterior cervical fusion with left fibular graft on 7/17/86 by Drs. Langford and Dunham. The patient postoperatively remained in his Philadelphia collar. However, on 7/21/86, postoperative day four, the patient developed some purulent drainage from his wound. He was started on antibiotics. Cultures were obtained showing Staph. epidermidis sensitive to Vancomycin. Infectious Disease recommended a month of Vancomycin treatment to try to keep him from developing osteomyelitis in his bone graft. The patient also had problems with low blood counts and his white blood cell count never really was raised by his infection. He received transfusions of packed red blood cells while he was in the hospital. He also had problems with IV infection in his left arm. This was improving and at the time of discharge was still sore with some redness. Repeat lateral C-spine showed the bone graft to be in good position and the fusion to be well done. He was followed in physical therapy and was able to ambulate well. On 7/29 the patient underwent placement of a Hickman catheter in order that he could go home on his Vancomycin IV treatment. The patient as discharged on 8/1/86 still febrile which probably was coming from his IV site, but it was felt that since the patient had been in the hospital a long time that he should go home, as the site was negative. He is to return to the neurosurgery clinic in one week, orthopedic clinic in two weeks and oncology clinic in two weeks.

Rhett Murray, M.D./sw

Addendum: Lab Studies And Progress Notes

DEPARTMENT OF RADIOLOGY REPORT 08/07/86 01:01

NAME: JIMERSON, RAYMOND *
DOB: 12/29/31
CASE NO.: 8945086217
MRN: 0526137
AGE/SEX: 054Y/M
SVC/CP: 07/80
LOCATION: U15E/1506
ADMITTED: 08/05/86
LOG DATE: 08/07/86
LOG TIME: 01:01
LOG I.D.: 05
ORDER #/EXAM: 0088644 CT SPINE THOR WO/CONTRAST 72128
PROC. CODE: 3056 72128
REF. PHYS.:
ADDRESS: 00000
ORD. PHYS.: LANGFORD KEITH H
ATT. PHYS.: LANGFORD KEITH H
? TO BE ANSWERED: CT TO FOLLOW EMERGENCY MYELOGRAM
HISTORY: METZ OF SPINE/PARALYSIS LOWER EXTREMITIES FX/T/9
PRIN. DIAGNOSIS:

GE 9800 THORACIC SPINE AND THORACOLUMBAR C.T.—WITH INTRATHECAL CONTRAST, 8/7/86

EXAMINATION & FINDINGS: The examination was performed on 8/7/86 and has just returned for interpretation. It appears that 10mm thickness was used for images which range from T1-2 level of L2-3 level.

Mixed osteolytic and osteoblastic metastases involve all demonstrated vertebrae. Myelography demonstrated severe compression of T9 vertebral body.

At T2 level there is localized left anterior extradural deformity which does not obliterate the subarachnoid space. At T3 level more severe extradural deformity is present anteriorly and laterally on the right. The subarachnoid space is still opacified however. There are mild to moderate extradural deformity at the T4-T6 levels. The most marked deformity here is present anterolaterally on the left at T5.

The portion of the examination which extends from T6 to L2-3 level was performed prior to contrast introduction. As noted above this shows mixed lytic-blastic involvement of all vertebrae. Myelography of the lumbar region and the caudal 6th thoracic vertebra reveals only extradural deformities which are difficult to differentiate from spondylosis.

IMPRESSION: (1) All demonstrated vertebrae show extensive osteolytic and osteoblastic metastatic involvement. (2) There is epidural compression of the thecal sac at T2 and T3 levels. However contrast passes through here. The subarachnoid space is adequately patent between T4 and T6 though there is evidence of epidural mass anterolaterally on the left at T5 level. (3) Severe compression of T9 vertebral body has been demonstrated by routine films and myelography.

8/15/86:jf

E.R. DUVALL M.D.
Personally Rendered By
(Radiologist)

Transcribed By _____
Resident _____
TECH ID: MARGARET A. ANDREWS

Addendum: Lab Studies And Progress Notes

The University of Alabama at Birmingham

PAGE 1

The Medical Center/University of Alabama Hospital

OPERATION NOTE

NAME: JIMERSON, RAYMOND MED.REC.NO.: 0526137 ROOM: 1530

SURG: Dr. Halpern ASSIST: Dr. Zamora

SURG.SIGN. _____

DATE OPER. 7/29/86 ADMITTED: DISCHARGED: 8-1

DOCTOR/SERV.: Dr. Norman Halpern DICTATED: 7/29/86 TRANSCRIBED: 7/29/86

DOCTOR/SERV.SIGN.: _____

PREOPERATIVE DIAGNOSIS: Osteomyelitis.

POSTOPERATIVE DIAGNOSIS: Same.

OPERATION: Placement of Hickman catheter.

FINDINGS: The right external jugular vein was good caliber and quality. The catheter initially snagged somewhere within the supraclavicular area but blind manipulation while waiting for fluoroscopy achieved good tip positioning without undue delay. The patient's position on the table, of course, was altered substantially by his inability to lie flat and the need to brace his neck and head because of the recent cervical spine operation. I think we were able to adequately prep our area away from any infection at the previous operative site. He tolerated the propped upright position without too much difficulty.

PROCEDURE: 0.5% lidocaine with epinephrine was used for infiltration anesthesia. A skin crease incision was made over the lower portion of the right external jugular vein which was readily identified. A stab wound was made in the mid right parasternal area and a subcutaneous tunnel was created from this point up toward the neck. The catheter was passed through the tunnel and the Dacron cuff was positioned appropriately. The catheter exit site was secured with vertical mattress sutures. The catheter was trimmed to an estimated fit and cannulated into the right external jugular vein. Fluoroscopy confirmed its tip position at the junction of the superior vena cava with the right atrium. The catheter was secured into the vein with 3-0 Dexon and aspiration and flushing were done easily. Betadine was used to irrigate the deep tissues.

The platysma was re-approximated with interrupted 3-0 Dexon, the skin was closed with interrupted subcuticular 4-0 Dexon. Appropriate dressings were applied to the neck and to the chest. Aspiration and flushing again were done. The catheter was filled with heparin/saline solution and was capped.

Norman Halpern, M. D./cw   cc: Keith Langford, M. D., UAB

† The Cross And Weeping Still †

Addendum: Lab Studies And Progress Notes

UAB — The University of Alabama at Birmingham

DEPARTMENT OF RADIOLOGY REPORT

08/05/86 22:53

```
NAME       JIMERSON, RAYMOND *           DOB 12/29/31           CASE NO. 8945086217
MRN        052613                        AGE/SEX 054Y/M         SVC/CP   07/80
LOCATION   UED /                                                ADMITTED 08/05/86
LOG DATE   08/05/86                      LOG TIME 22:53         LOG I.D. 08
ORDER #/EXAM 0088081  SPINE CERVICAL MIN 4 VWS 72050            PROC. CODE 3050 72050
REF. PHYS. DR LANGFORD,
ADDRESS                                  00000
ORD. PHYS. PRIEST      MARLON   L        ATT. PHYS. PRIEST      MARLON   L
? TO BE ANSWERED R/O FX

HISTORY         54YOBM POST CERVICAL FUSION
PRIN. DIAGNOSIS DIAGNOSIS NOT CODED
```

Status post posterior fusion of C3 through C6. Compression fracture of C4 and C5. Bony fragments project posteriorly 4mm at C4 and C5 level.

8-6-86ash   S.Dalton,M.D./1713
S.Friedman,MD.

Transcribed By _____   Personally Rendered By _____
Resident _____   (Radiologist)
                                 TECH ID: BILLY HUGHES

Addendum: Lab Studies And Progress Notes

The University of Alabama at Birmingham   PAGE 2

The Medical Center/University of Alabama Hospital

OPERATION NOTE

NAME: JIMERSON, RAYMOND   MED.REC.NO.: 0526137 ROOM:

An incision had been made over the posterior iliac crest but down to the posterior ilium. The bone in this area was too soft to use as a support bone graft. Therefore, the area was closed with 2-0 Vicryl and 3-0 nylon in the skin.

The patient tolerated the procedure well, went to the recovery room in good condition.

W. K. Dunham, M. D./cw

Addendum: Lab Studies And Progress Notes

The University of Alabama at Birmingham
The Medical Center/University of Alabama Hospital

PAGE 1

OPERATION NOTE

NAME: JIMERSON, RAYMOND MED.REC.NO.: 0526137 ROOM: 1530

SURG: Dr. Dunham and Dr. Langford ASSIST: Dr. Tim Cool and Dr. C. Morris

SURG.SIGN.: *[signature]*

DATE OPER. 7/17/86 ADMITTED: DISCHARGED: 8-1

DOCTOR/SERV.: Dr. W. K. Dunham DICTATED: 7/17/86 TRANSCRIBED: 7/17/86

DOCTOR/SERV.SIGN.: *[signature]*

PREOPERATIVE DIAGNOSIS: Metastatic carcinoma of the prostate; collapsed cervical spine; unstable cervical spine.

POSTOPERATIVE DIAGNOSIS: Same.

OPERATION: Posterior wiring and fusion, C3-4-5 and 6, using fibular graft from left leg.

COMMENT: Doctor Langford accomplished the exposure and he will dictate that part of the procedure.

Next, we stripped the periosteum away from the posterior elements, cleared all soft tissue from the spinous processes of C3 through C6. We then took an 18 gauge wire and passed it through the base of the spinous process of C3. This was then taken underneath the spinous process of C6. Next, using the towel clip, the Lewin clamp and the breast tenaculum, the 18 gauge wire was passed through the spinous process of C4, then around through C5 and under C6 and then looped back on itself and tightened by twisting. The two wires then securely fixed C3 to C6. Next, the fibula was harvested from the left leg through a straight lateral incision, going between the anterior and the lateral compartments of the leg. It was cut with oscillating saw. A segment 2.5 inches long was then split longitudinally with the saw and drill holes were made with the Hall drill. Next, these two hemisected pieces of fibula were inserted beside the spinous processes of C3 to 6 and then wires were passed under the wires between spinous processes and through the holes in the hemisected fibula. These were then tightened sequentially. A third wire was placed across the superior aspect at the base of C3 and through around the hemisected fibula at the superior aspect of the fusion. When these three wires were tightened, this added additional stability to the entire construct. The wound was irrigated with antibacterial solution. X-rays were taken that showed good position of the wires, the fracture and the fibular grafts. A 2507 Hemovac was placed in. Layer-by-layer closure with 0 Vicryl, 2-0 Vicryl was carried out. The fibula was closed with 0 Vicryl and skin staples.

Addendum: Lab Studies And Progress Notes

The University of Alabama at Birmingham   PAGE 1

The Medical Center/University of Alabama Hospital

OPERATION NOTE

NAME: JIMERSON, RAYMOND   MED.REC.NO.: 0526137 ROOM: 1530

SURG: Dr. Langford   ASSIST: Dr. Murray in association with
SURG.SIGN. _____   Dr. Dunham and Dr. Cool

DATE OPER. 7/17/86   ADMITTED: DISCHARGED:

DOCTOR/SERV.: Dr. Keith Langford   DICTATED: 7/17/86   TRANSCRIBED: 7/17/86
DOCTOR/SERV.SIGN.: _____

PREOPERATIVE DIAGNOSIS: Metastatic carcinoma of the prostate; collapsed cervical spine; unstable cervical spine.

POSTOPERATIVE DIAGNOSIS:

OPERATION: Posterior wiring and fusion, C3-4-5 and 6, using fibular graft from left leg.

COMMENT: This unfortunate man had been troubled by neck pain and neck x-ray had shown that there was a collapse of the central vertebral spine with angulation forward almost to right angle. The amazing thing was that he appeared to have no neurological deficit and when put in traction, the neckline straightened out. It was quite clear that the interspinous ligaments had become extremely loose in the process of the cervical spine collapse and between C4 and 5 and C5 and 6 was the biggest gap, suggesting that the major instability was at C4-5-6 but we reasoned that C3 would need to be included in the wiring and fusion to get the maximum stability.

The surgery was done without any major incident but, unfortunately, we did find tumor involving the left lateral masses of C3 and C4 and there was tumor extending out and destroying bone in that area. Bleeding occurred from that but not in any torrential amount and it was controlled with Avitene.

The total loss of blood was only about 300 cc.

An attempt was made to harvest bone from the right iliac crest but this patient has had radiation to the iliac bones and so we were not prepared to use that. As stability was the major object, fibular bone was eventually chosen for the graft.

After the spines and laminae from C2 to C6 had been stripped of soft tissue, we handed the case over to Doctor Dunham but provided holes through the bases of the spine of C3-4-5.

Addendum: Lab Studies And Progress Notes

The University of Alabama at Birmingham   PAGE 2

The Medical Center/University of Alabama Hospital

OPERATION NOTE

NAME: JIMERSON, RAYMOND   MED.REC.NO.: 0526137   ROOM:

PROCEDURE: With the patient prone on the headrest, a lateral C-spine was taken which showed that the neck alignment was good and then an incision was made through the skin which was folded in a most awkward fashion and provided difficulty for us in getting access.

After the cut was taken down to the spines, we had a little difficulty identifying C2 and 3 which were in very close opposition as it turned out, and a lateral C-spine was again taken to identify C3. The towel clip was found to be between C3 and 4.

The stripping of muscles and ligaments was done very carefully because of the possibility that tumor did involve the lateral masses as it turned out to be the case and in that fashion, we avoided any major bleeding.

The dissection was carried out to the facet joints and then using curets, coagulation and small nibblers, we removed the soft tissue piecemeal between C2 and 3, C3 and 4, C4 and 5 and C5 and 6.

Holes were punched through the base of the spines using towel clips, breast tenaculum and, in one case, the Lewin clamp.

A size 18 gauge wire was put through the base of the spine of C3. At that time, Doctor Dunham took over. The wound was closed by Doctor Dunham and Doctor Cool.

It remains to be said that at the time he was put to sleep, he was already prone and had been moving his hands and feet well. Nothing occurred during surgery to indicate that there was any injury to the spinal cord and we hope that there will be no complications other than that related to his tumor.

Keith Langford, M. D./cw

Addendum: Lab Studies And Progress Notes

The University of Alabama at Birmingham　　　　　　　　　　　PAGE 1

The Medical Center/University of Alabama Hospital

DISCHARGE SUMMARY

NAME: JIMERSON, RAYMOND　　　　　　MED.REC.NO. 0526137　ROOM: 1530

DOCTOR/SERV.: Keith Langford, M.D./0974　ADMITTED: 7/13/86　DISCHARGED: 8/1/86

　　　　　　　　　　　　　　　　　　　DICTATED: 8/1/86　TRANSCRIBED: 8/6/86

PRIMARY DIAGNOSES:　　　　　Collapse of cervical vertebra.
　　　　　　　　　　　　　　Metastatic and prostate carcinoma.
　　　　　　　　　　　　　　Osteomyelitis.
　　　　　　　　　　　　　　Wound infection.
　　　　　　　　　　　　　　Anemia of chronic disease.
　　　　　　　　　　　　　　Hickman catheter placement.

PRIMARY PROCEDURE:　　　　　Cervical fusion with autogenous bone graft and wiring
　　　　　　　　　　　　　　posteriorly 7/17/86.
　　　　　　　　　　　　　　Packed cell transfusion, multiple.

FOLLOW UP:　　　　　　　　　Return to clinic in two weeks, oncology clinic in two
　　　　　　　　　　　　　　weeks, Dr. Langford's neurosurgery clinic in one week.

DISCHARGE MEDICATIONS:　　　Tylenol #3; diazepam, 5 mg. p.o.; Vancomycin, 1 gram
　　　　　　　　　　　　　　q.12h. by IV line.

DISPOSITION:　　　　　　　　Discharged to home.

HISTORY OF PRESENT ILLNESS: The patient was admitted on 7/13/86, one of several UAH admissions for this 54 YOBM with prostatic adenocarcinoma metastatic to bone. He presented in 10/84 with low back pain and workup revealed prostatic cancer with lumbar metastasis. Initial treatment was DES at 1 mg. t.i.d. and subsequently increased to 4 mg. q.day for worsening back pain with complete resolution of pain. He also received radiation therapy L1-3 and left hemipelvis. In 2/86 the patient referred himself to Dr. Lobuglio. Acid phosphatase was 17. Bone scan demonstrated increased uptake in the thoracic lumbar vertebra, ribs, femur, humerus and pelvis. _____, 1 mg. daily was added to his treatment regimen. The patient was hospitalized from 5-6 to 5-14 for urinary incontinence. Post void residual was negative. Cystoureterogram with no results available. Myelogram showed diffuse mets from T9 to 12 with extradural compression from tumor and mild disk disease from L3 to S1. Radiation oncology initiated treatment to the axial skeleton C7-S1. Ultimate impression of neurology and neurosurgery was that the patient had cauda equina syndrome and thus the sacral roots were added to radiation field. During hospitalization the patient also developed left shoulder pain. X-rays revealed metastasis to the left proximal humerus. The patient was discharged on 5/14 and has been doing generally well at home. He was seen in clinic on 7/11/86 and felt to be doing well. He came to the UAH Emergency Department complaining of soreness in his shoulder. Cervical and thoracic films revealed new compression fractures from

Addendum: Lab Studies And Progress Notes

the University of Alabama in Birmingham
the Medical Center / UNIVERSITY OF ALABAMA HOSPITAL

JIMERSON, RAYMOND
122931 52212 07/13/86
054Y KNM BAP 052 61 37
DR PRIEST   MARLON
JRN

HISTORY, PHYSICAL EXAMINATION AND PROGRESS NOTES

NOTES

fractures of C3+5 T3 & T9. He is to be admitted to the Oncology Service for stabilisation of his spine and for evaluation by Rad-Onc service.

PMHx unremarkable
   Meds: Leuprolide & DES   Allergies: Motrin

FH, SH, ROS - noncontributory.

PE Young- for-stated-age black male in no acute distress
BP-150/90 P-92 RR-18 T-98
Skin - ∅ rash   Nodes - ∅   HEENT - NC/AT; EOM's full; sclerae anicteric; P²¾ NRL; mouth ∅ lesions   NECK - cervical collar - thyroid not examined. Chest-clear COR - RRR s̄ (m) Abd - soft, nontender, BS ⊕, organomegaly; Neuro - CN's II→XII intact; CEREBELL ⊕ FTN; SENS - ⊕ PP, proprio; STRENGTH - 5+/5+ all extremities DTR's [reflex diagram] Gait - not assessed

Data Base - pending   C-spine/T-spine → see HPI

Imp/Plan
1) Metastatic Prostate Ca → Bone c̄ Unstable C/T spine & new fx's. Will place traction & stabilise pt; admit to floor; obtain complete adm profile (attn Ca⁺⁺, Phos); complete bedrest; SQ Heparin prophylaxis; Rad Onc consult for addnl RT in AM. Neurosurgery has seen pt & agrees c̄ plan.

EKHawes M.D.
JAmos Bailey

FORM N-12 REV. 6-64 PAGE 2

Addendum: Lab Studies And Progress Notes

LLOYD NOLAND EMERGENCY DEPARTMENT RECORD

... AUTHORIZATION FOR TREATMENT ...

THE UNDERSIGNED HEREBY GRANTS AUTHORIZATION FOR SUCH TREATMENT AND PROCEDURES CONSIDERED NECESSARY FOR THE PATIENT WHOSE NAME APPEARS AT THE BOTTOM OF THIS PAGE. THE UNDERSIGNED IS AWARE OF THIS AUTHORIZATION AND CERTIFIES THAT NO GUARANTEE OR ASSURANCE HAS BEEN MADE AS TO THE RESULTS THAT MAY BE OBTAINED.

DATE: 11-9-86 TIME: 10:38 A.M. SIGNED: Vertie K. Jimerson (wife)
WITNESS: Pat Bush
(AUTHORIZED PERSON AND RELATIONSHIP)

FORM OF ARRIVAL: ☒ AMBULANCE

HOW INJURED / OR CHIEF COMPLAINT: fever, prostatic CA c̄ pain

T: 100° P: 132 R: 28 B.P: 116/90 AGE: 54 WHERE INJURED: ☒ OTHER
ALLERGY: NKA   TET/DIPTET: 86   MISC: foley cath, hickman cath
TRIAGE TIME: 10:44 A.M. ROOM NO: 24 TIME: 10:44 SIGNATURE: Davidson

CURRENT MEDICATIONS: MS 20mg po 1½-2 hrs, sorbitol, percodan, flexeril, Nolvadex, decadron 2mg qd, Valium 5mg bid, ultracef, ???, haldol hs

HISTORY AND PHYSICAL:

S — Pt c̄ metastatic CA of prostate has developed intractable pain over the past few days. He previously was getting good relief c̄ oral morphine but now is taking 20mg every 1½-2 hrs. S/E b/f. He also has pretty much stopped eating, although the wife has been able to get a little forced down him. He also has had fever — has some mild fever almost all the time but has been up to 102° the last couple days. His urine grew E. coli & Pseudomonas during last hospitalization.

O — Pt moaning almost constantly, does not verbally respond. HEENT — unremarkable for acute process.

IMPRESSION: UTI c̄ sepsis; intractable pain   RTW:

X-RAY LAB RESULTS
1. cath U/A
2. urine C&S
3. CBC
4. blood cultures x2
5. SMA6

ASSESSMENT / MEDICATION / TREATMENT
1. lungs — basilar rales
2. heart sounds obscured by moaning
3. abdomen - soft
4. urine in foley bag appear grossly infected
5.

INSTRUCTIONS (MUST BE DONE ON THIS SIDE) WRITE COMPLETE SENTENCES AND LIST DRUGS PRESCRIBED

Pt transferred to floor with Admit medicine Dr. Pineda. Notify on arrival to floor.

PHYSICIAN'S SIGNATURE: C. ??? Nelson M.D.

DISPOSITION DISCHARGE ___ ADMITTED 11:57 A.M. DIC/DOA ___ CONDITION: ☒ G ☒ F ☐ S
205-B   D. ??? R.N.

NAME: Raymond Jimerson
MEDICAL RECORD NO: 08-68-02

I Have Received and Understand The Above Instructions.
PATIENT'S SIGNATURE

Addendum: Lab Studies And Progress Notes

LLOYD NOLAND HOSPITAL & HEALTH CENTERS

MEDICINE CLINIC 11/5/86

DIAGNOSIS: Prostatic carcinoma.

Mr. Jimerson has been brought in today by his wife. They have elected to go ahead and get transfusion today. He was given three units of packed red blood cells without any complications. His temperature on admission today was 102°F. This usually happens whenever the manipulation of the Foley catheter is on. She had irrigated today. Apparently the temperature comes down as soon as the full irrigation is taken care of. We had advised Mrs. Jimerson as to the proper utilization of Haldol and Benedryl combination which apparently has helped significantly his mental status.

Raymond Jimerson
08 68 02

Luis Pineda, M.D./et

MEDICINE CLINIC 11 4 86

DIAGNOSIS:

S: I have been contacted by Ms. Jimerson who states that Mr. Jimerson is not doing any better. Apparently he is extremely pale and she wonders about the possibility of transfusing him.

HGB 6.3 grams%, HCT 19%, white count 6,700 with normal differential. Nucleated cells and left shift is present. Platelet count 127,000.

P: We will go ahead as such and set up transfusion. We will try to obtain this through the Hospice Department of Jefferson County. If not we will go ahead and bring him in for out patient blood transfusion.

Raymond Jimerson
MR #08-68-02

Luis Pineda, M.D./jt-b

220B

HISTORY AND PHYSICAL SHEET
AND/OR PROGRESS NOTE RECORD

Addendum: Lab Studies And Progress Notes

† The Cross And Weeping Still †

LLOYD NO[RLAN]D EMERGENCY DEPARTMENT R[EC]ORD
... AUTHORIZATION FOR TREATMENT ...

THE UNDERSIGNED HEREBY GRANTS AUTHORIZATION FOR SUCH TREATMENT AND PROCEDURES CONSIDERED NECESSARY FOR THE PATIENT WHOSE NAME APPEARS AT THE BOTTOM OF THIS PAGE. THE UNDERSIGNED IS AWARE OF THIS AUTHORIZATION AND CERTIFIES THAT NO GUARANTEE OR ASSURANCE HAS BEEN MADE AS TO THE RESULTS THAT MAY BE OBTAINED.

DATE: 9-18-96 TIME: 10:03 A.M. SIGNATURE: X _____
WITNESS: C. Kilgore (AUTHORIZED PERSON AND RELATIONSHIP)
FORM OF ARRIVAL: ☐ CAR ☒ AMBULANCE ☐ OTHER _____
HOW INJURED / OR CHIEF COMPLAINT: Fever 104°

T: 103.9 B: 132 R: 24 B.P.: 114/8 AGE: 54 WHERE INJURED: ☐ HOME ☐ WORK ☐ OTHER N/A
ALLERGY: NKA TT/DIPTET: _ MISC: N/A
TRIAGE TIME: 10:12 A.M. ROOM NO. 130 TIME: 10:02 SIGNATURE: J. Ford
CURRENT MEDICATIONS: Nolvadex, Percodan

HISTORY AND PHYSICAL: NO OV CHART AVAILABLE
54 y.o. BM presents c/o fever consult with x- prostate bad
Chemotherapy - pt has history prostate CA [?]

54 y.o BM in ??
A+O clear Hickman catheter in place
RL NL
ABD soft

IMPRESSION: ① Fever ② Neutropenia RTW: _

X-RAY LAB RESULTS	ASSESSMENT / MEDICATION / TREATMENT
1. CBC WBC 2000 Hgb 10.8 Hct 31	Plt <100,000 P62 S14 10L
2. SMA ??	2.
3. CXR N- definite infiltrate	3.
4. UA ??	4.
5. Blood Cultures x2	5.

INSTRUCTIONS (MUST BE DONE ON THIS SIDE) WRITE COMPLETE SENTENCES AND LIST DRUGS PRESCRIBED

Admit to Dr. Pineda

PHYSICIAN'S SIGNATURE: R.T. Boyer, M.D.

DISPOSITION: DISCHARGE ___ ADMITTED 1010 A.M. DIC/DOA ___ CONDITION: ___ OF ___ R.N.
NAME: Raymond Timerson
MEDICAL RECORD NO.: 08-68-03
I Have Received and Understand The Above Instructions
PATIENT'S SIGNATURE

Addendum: Lab Studies And Progress Notes

Baptist Medical Centers
X-RAY REQUISITION

DATE 9-4-85

X-Ray No. _____ Tech _____ NAME _____ DOCTOR _____

Ambulatory _____ Ck'd by _____
Wheelchair _____
Stretcher _____ 1/9/5/85 ROOM
Portable _____
Previous X-Ray ___ yes ___ no   Radiologist

JIMERSON RAYMOND SR
MCLEAN DR BARRY 09/04/85
834166 DC   0695C

RADIOLOGIC EXAMINATION OF Bone Scan, Today
"Hr Stage Cyposhte, chose
compare to previous scan

X-Ray Service Code
1288306
1262170
1261100

PATIENT HAZARD REMINDER

Clinical Diagnosis & Remarks: metastatic Prostate cancer

X-Ray Treatment For _____
Service of Dr. _____ Intern/Resident _____ Nurse _____

JIMERSON   RADIOLOGIC AND FLUOROSCOPIC FINDINGS
9/5/85

BONE SCAN: 22 mCi of 99m Tc MDP were used for the study.

Recheck examination again shows focal areas of increased isotope activity throughout the spine and ribs, improved compared to 10/11/84. There is less focal isotope activity in the pelvis now including the hips. There are some focal areas of increased isotope activity in the skull which are unchanged. There is less focal isotope activity in the shoulders. There is less focal isotope activity in the sternum.

OPINION: Diffuse skeletal metastasis as described, improved compared to 10/11/84.

PELVIS, AP: Osteoblastic metastasis is seen throughout the pelvis, essentially the same as on the study of 10/11/84.

AP CHEST FOR RIB DETAIL: Osteoblastic activity throughout the ribs is noted.

HM VAUGHN, MD/plc

Radiologist _____

Addendum: Lab Studies And Progress Notes

LLOYD NOLAND HOSPITAL
WRITE FIRMLY — USE BALL POINT

RECORD: Patient's Progress, Pertinent Observations, and Nursing Intervention
(SIGN ALL ENTRIES)

DATE	TIME	
9-19-86		Pt admitted to 224 B, Dr. Pineda. Transported to floor per stretcher. — T. Marrow

Raymond Jamerson
Chart # 08622
Acct # 336680

NURSES' PROGRESS NOTES

Addendum: Lab Studies And Progress Notes

The University of Alabama at Birmingham PAGE 1
The Medical Center/University of Alabama Hospital

DISCHARGE SUMMARY

NAME: JIMERSON, RAYMOND   MED.REC.NO. 0526137   ROOM: 1506

DOCTOR/SERV.: Keith Langford, M.D./0974   ADMITTED: 8/5/86   DISCHARGED: 8/15/86

DICTATED: 8/18/86   TRANSCRIBED: 8/22/86

PRIMARY DIAGNOSIS: Metastatic prostate cancer. Spinal cord injury secondary to fracture, metastic disease.

PRIMARY PROCEDURE: CAT scan irradiation therapy.

SUMMARY: This is a 54 YOBM with known metastatic prostate cancer who was status post cervical effusion in mid July by Dr. Langford for collapsed vertebra, C4. He had been neurologically intact at that time and had been discharged on 8/1/86. He was walking up some steps and felt his legs go out from under him. Since then he has been unable to walk. He denies any pain and he retains sensation in his lower extremites. He has also been unable to void for about twelve hours and on arrival to UAB ER he was catheterized with about 800 cc. urine returning. He has a Hickman catheter in and is on home vancomycin for septic phlebitis from previous hospital stay.

PHYSICAL EXAMINATION: He was found to have no rectal tone. He had 2/5 hip abductors, hamstring, quads, gastrocs and tibialis anterior function on the left; no function on the right in the lower extremity. His sensation was intact to pinprick. Position sense was also intact. His toes were neutral. There were no deep tendon reflexes elicited in either lower extremity. The C-spine films showed the fusion to be intact with no displacement. Thoracic spine films showed a compression fracture C9, lumbar spine was okay.

HOSPITAL COURSE: The patient was admitted and a thoracolumbar myelogram was performed. There were multiple bony mets seen and there was block at T3 level due to tumor. Radiation therapy was consulted and they began radiation treatment. During his stay he improved only slightly in his neurologic function. He did receive a course of radiation therapy. He requested to see the medical oncologist who were to offer him choice concerning the appropriateness of chemotherapy for his cancer. This will be followed up on an outpatient basis. He was discharged home on 8/15/86. Medications: He was given Percodan for pain and will complete his radiation therapy as an outpatient. He will see Dr. Langford in one month.

Mark Scofield, M.D./sw

† The Cross And Weeping Still †

Addendum: Lab Studies And Progress Notes

```
UAB                    DEPARTMENT OF RADIOLOGY REPORT           08/05/86 22:52
The University of Alabama at Birmingham

      NAME  JIMERSON, RAYMOND *          DOB 12/29/31         CASE NO. 8945066217
       MRN  052613                       AGE/SEX 054Y/M       SVC/CP  07/80
  LOCATION  UED /                                             ADMITTED 08/05/86
  LOG DATE  08/05/86                     LOG TIME 22:52       LOG I.D. 08
ORDER #/EXAM 0088082   SPINE THORACIC AP&L/SWMRS72072         PROC. CODE 3050 72072
 REF. PHYS.  DR LANGFORD,
    ADDRESS                                    00000
  ORD. PHYS. PRIEST       MARLON    L     ATT. PHYS. PRIEST      MARLON    L
? TO BE ANSWERED R/O FX

   HISTORY  54YOBM POST SPINAL FUSION
PRIN. DIAGNOSIS DIAGNOSIS NOT CODED


        Widespread metastatic disease. Compression fracture T9.

        8-6-86ash/S.Friedman,MD.              S.Dalton,M.D./1713
```

Transcribed By _____ Personally Rendered By _____
                                                                    (Radiologist)
Resident _____   TECH ID BILLY HUGHES

www.ingramcontent.com/pod-product-compliance
Lightning Source LLC
Chambersburg PA
CBHW080443110426
42743CB00016B/3260